Frommer's™

Valencia
day BY day™

1st Edition

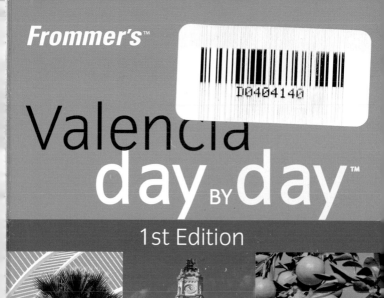

by Timothy-V. Birch

WILEY

A John Wiley and Sons, Ltd, Publication

Contents

Cardin 7061

UK Publisher: Sally Smith
Executive Project Editor: Daniel Mersey
Commissioning Editor: Fiona Quinn
Development Editor: Karen Fitzpatrick
Content Editor: Erica Peters
Cartography: SY Cartography
Photo Research: Jill Emeny

Wiley also publishes its books in a variety of electronic formats. Some
content that appears in print may not be available in electronic books.

British Library Cataloguing in Publication Data

A catalogue record for this book is available from the British Library

ISBN: 978-0-470-72170-4

Typeset by Wiley Indianapolis Composition Services

Printed and bound in China by RR Donnelley

5 4 3 2 1

A Note from the Editorial Director

Organizing your time. That's what this guide is all about.

Other guides give you long lists of things to see and do and then expect you to fit the pieces together. The Day by Day guides are different. These guides tell you the best of everything, and then they show you how to see it *in the smartest, most time-efficient way*. Our authors have designed detailed itineraries organized by time, neighborhood, or special interest. And each tour comes with a bulleted map that takes you from stop to stop.

Hoping to explore the Centro Histórico, the space-age architecture of the City of Arts and Sciences or eat paella Valenciana in the Albufera, where it was invented? Planning a day by the beach with the kids? Whatever your interest or schedule, the Day by Days give you the smartest routes to follow. Not only do we take you to the top attractions, hotels, and restaurants, but we also help you access those special moments that locals get to experience—those "finds" that turn tourists into travelers.

The Day by Days are also your top choice if you're looking for one complete guide for all your travel needs. The best hotels and restaurants for every budget, the greatest shopping values, the wildest nightlife—it's all here.

Why should you trust our judgment? Because our authors personally visit each place they write about. They're an independent lot who say what they think and would never include places they wouldn't recommend to their best friends. They're also open to suggestions from readers. If you'd like to contact them, please send your comments our way at feedback@frommers.com, and we'll pass them on.

Enjoy your Day by Day guide—the most helpful travel companion you can buy. And have the trip of a lifetime.

Warm regards,

Kelly Regan

Kelly Regan, Editorial Director
Frommer's Travel Guides

About the Author

Timothy-V. Birch was born in London and almost immediately moved with his airline company family to Beirut, Lebanon. He spent the next 18 years of his life traveling around the globe whenever his father was reposted. He joined the airlines himself, following in his father's footsteps, ending with several years at Iberia, designing publicity material, and writing copy and fell in love with Spain. He left the airlines in the late eighties to set up a greeting card and fine art print publishing house with his wife Diana, selling designs based on his own work. In 1999, they moved permanently to Valencia with their two young daughters. Tim and Diana live in the center of Valencia, with their daughters as neighbors just a few streets away. They have a comprehensive website, www.thisisvalencia.com, about the city, both for visitors and residents. Tim writes about the city and the area for various publications around the world and has promised his wife he will start painting again very soon.

Acknowledgments

So many people to thank in my life, but heartfelt thanks to the three most important people in my life; my muses and my very best friends, Diana my wife, and my daughters Poppy and Lilly. To my late parents for giving me the wanderlust in the first place. To our family and friends both here in Valencia and abroad for their loyal friendship and untiring love and support through the years. To Barbara and Mike, Wolf and Therese, Sally and Terry, and Miles and Ingrid for their encouragement, particularly during the writing of this book and, finally to Fiona at Frommer's and Karen Fitzpatrick for helping me write better, less, and more!

An Additional Note

Please be advised that travel information is subject to change at any time—and this is especially true of prices. We therefore suggest that you write or call ahead for confirmation when making your travel plans. The authors, editors, and publisher cannot be held responsible for the experiences of readers while traveling. Your safety is important to us, however, so we encourage you to stay alert and be aware of your surroundings.

Star Ratings, Icons & Abbreviations

Every hotel, restaurant, and attraction listing in this guide has been ranked for quality, value, service, amenities, and special features using a **star-rating system.** Hotels, restaurants, attractions, shopping, and nightlife are rated on a scale of zero stars (recommended) to three stars (exceptional). In addition to the star-rating system, we also use a **kids icon** to point out the best bets for families. Within each tour, we recommend cafes, bars or restaurants where you can take a break. Each of these stops appears in a shaded box marked with a coffee cup–shaped bullet 🍵 .

The following **abbreviations** are used for credit cards:

AE	American Express	DISC	Discover	V	Visa
DC	Diners Club	MC	MasterCard		

Frommers.com

Now that you have this guidebook to help you plan a great trip, visit our website at **www.frommers.com** for additional travel information on more than 4,000 destinations. We update features regularly to give you instant access to the most current trip-planning information available. At Frommers.com, you'll find scoops on the best airfares, lodging rates, and car rental bargains. You can even book your travel online through our reliable travel booking partners.

A Note on Prices

In the "Take a Break" and "Best Bets" sections of this book, we have used a system of dollar signs to show a range of costs for 1 night in a hotel (the price of a double-occupancy room) or the cost of an entree (main meal) at a restaurant. Use the following table to decipher the dollar signs:

Cost	Hotels	Restaurants
$	under $100	under $10
$$	$100–$200	$10–$20
$$$	$200–$300	$20–$30
$$$$	$300–$400	$30–$40
$$$$$	over $400	over $40

An Invitation to the Reader

In researching this book, we discovered many wonderful places—hotels, restaurants, shops, and more. We're sure you'll find others. Please tell us about them, so we can share the information with your fellow travelers in upcoming editions. If you were disappointed with a recommendation, we'd love to know that, too. Please write to:

Frommer's Valencia Day by Day, 1st Edition
Wiley Publishing, Inc. • 111 River St. • Hoboken, NJ 07030-5774

12 Favorite
Moments

12 Favorite Moments

1. Plaza de la Virgen
2. Plaza Santa Catalina
3. La Catedral
4. Mercado Central
5. Albufera
6. Malvarossa Beach
7. L'Oceanogràfic
8. Museo de Bellas Artes
9. Ayuntamiento
10. Calle San Vicente
11. 39º 27N
12. Casa-Museo José Benlliure

(i) Information
✉ Post Office
Ⓜ Metro Station

0   1/4 mi
0   0.25 km

Not long ago Valencia was unknown as a tourist destination. Six or seven years ago, many would have been unsure whether it was in Italy or Spain. Spain's third largest city is beginning to overtake Barcelona in the popularity polls—quite an achievement. I love the city for many reasons; here are 12 of my favorites.

① **Joining the crowds to watch the Virgin arriving in Plaza de la Virgen.** The Basilica is home to a gilt statue of La Virgen de las Desamporados (Virgin of the Deserted). Occasionally she is lifted from her resting place, put in a specially constructed glass-sided van, and taken to another church in the area. Carried by strong men, crowds gather to bid her farewell or welcome her home. *See p 29.*

② **Sipping horchata and nibbling on fartons.** Made from *chufa* (tiger nuts), *horchata* is a locally produced sweet drink, served icy cold with warm *fartons*, sticky finger-buns for dunking. The combination is refreshing, delicious, and an obsession here. The best place to enjoy them is in the Plaza Santa Catalina. *See p 27.*

③ **Strolling around the city in the early morning.** Valencians live for the night, often playing until dawn. The city is usually deserted around 8am—an ideal time to take photos with no one to distract the view of the Catedral. *See p 27.*

④ **Admiring the Art Nouveau of the Mercado Central.** The magnificent central market is said to be the largest in Europe. We like to get a coffee and *tostadas* (toast with olive oil and salt) for breakfast at the bar and watch the market getting under way while taking in the detail of this exquisite mosaic building. *See p 9.*

⑤ **Watching the sunset on the Albufera.** A short bus ride brings you to this tranquil lake where

Mercado Central.

Sunset over the Albufera.

watching the waterfowl at sunset is so calming. Amazing to think you are only 10 minutes from the city center. *See p 84.*

❻ Having paella on Malvarossa Beach. Just to the north of the port is Paseo Neptuno, where restaurants famous for paella and seafood line the promenade. There is nothing more pleasurable than spending an afternoon sharing paella with friends. *See p 14.*

❼ Marveling at the L'Oceanogràfic's tropical fish room. Europe's largest aquarium has a captivating tropical fish room with boat-shaped benches and chillout music. It's particularly soothing—and it's surprising how often you have the room to yourself. *See p 25.*

❽ Spending Sunday afternoon at the Museo de Bellas Artes. The city's museums are free on a Sunday. I love the Museo de Bellas Artes. Go around 2pm when the locals are enjoying their Sunday family paellas: you'll have the place to yourselves. *See p 39.*

❾ Kickstarting the day with a Carajillo. Spanish coffee is notoriously strong and a *carajillo* really packs a punch. It's an espresso with more-than-a-dash of liquor, taken early morning to kick-start the

day—very Valencian. Best enjoyed with the locals in one of the bars off the Ayuntamiento. *See p 123.*

❿ Being moved by the Ofrenda at Las Fallas. This is the devotional side of Las Fallas. Watching more than 100,000 traditionally dressed Falleras parading through the streets with flowers to decorate the huge effigy of The Virgin is very moving and beautiful, particularly on Calle San Vicente as they near the end of their long walk. *See p 123.*

⓫ Enjoying a little beer at 39°27N. A nice Spanish habit is the tapa, a modest dish of something to eat with your drink. A *caña* is just enough to quench your thirst. Have one at 39°27N opposite Port America's Cup with a *tapa* of *patatas bravas*. But beware, they can be fiery. *See p 105.*

⓬ Escaping to a secret garden. Sometimes, to escape the occasionally ferocious heat of summer, I go to the enchanting Casa-Museo José Benlliure and sit in the shade of the delightful garden. It's often several degrees cooler than elsewhere, and so very peaceful. Afterwards I like to visit the artist's Aladdin's cave of a studio, left as though he had just walked away for a few moments. *See p 18.* ●

The Ofrenda at night.

The Best
Full-Day Tours

The Best **in One Day**

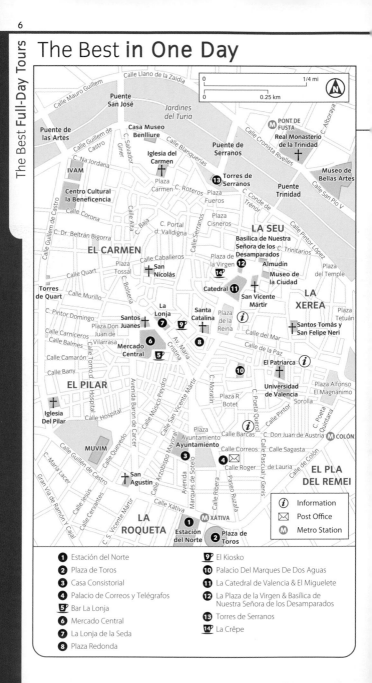

1. Estación del Norte
2. Plaza de Toros
3. Casa Consistorial
4. Palacio de Correos y Telégrafos
5. Bar La Lonja
6. Mercado Central
7. La Lonja de la Seda
8. Plaza Redonda
9. El Kiosko
10. Palacio Del Marques De Dos Aguas
11. La Catedral de Valencia & El Miguelete
12. La Plaza de la Virgen & Basílica de Nuestra Señora de los Desamparados
13. Torres de Serranos
14. La Crêpe

The joy of Valencia is that you can easily discover the best of it on foot in just one day—but wear a good pair of shoes! This tour mostly takes place within the mercifully flat *Centro Histórico*. It starts at the *Modernista* masterpiece Estación del Norte and ends by the Torres de Serranos, one of the two remaining gates to the original walled city. START: **Metro to Xàtiva or bus 5, 6, 7, 8, 19, 35 or 40.**

❶ ★ kids Estación del Norte. Valencian-born Demetrio Ribes (1877–1921), one of the most important Modernista architects of his time, designed this wonderful building in the 'Sezesión Vienesa' style. Designed in 1906 and completed in 1917, this busy main railway station is decorated on the outside with ceramic oranges and delightful mosaics depicting local scenes. Inside, the ticket hall is all dark woods and white mosaics with gold leafed 'Bon Voyage' messages in a multitude of languages. ⏲ *20 min. C/ Xàtiva 24.* ☎ *96-352-0202. www.renfe.es. Daily 5am–2am. Metro: Xàtiva.*

Mosaic on the façade of Estación del Norte.

Statue of a Matador, Plaza de Toros.

❷ ★ kids Plaza de Toros. Just next door, the Bullring has been home to Valencian bullfights for more than 150 years. Designed by Sebastián Monleón (1815–1875) in 1851, it is a 48-sided polygon surrounding a 52m/170ft bullring, and has a capacity of 16,000. Bullfights take place during fiestas, usually about three times a year (see p 155). At other times, it is used for exhibitions and concerts. Visit the Museo Taurino for a view into the ring. ⏲ *15 min. C/ Xàtiva 6.* ☎ *96-351-9315 www.museotaurino valencia.es. Admission free. Tues–Sun 10am–8pm. Metro: Xàtiva.*

❸ ★★ Casa Consistorial. The city's Town Hall, or Casa Consistorial, dominates one side of the Plaza

Ayuntamiento lit up at night.

Ayuntamiento. A splendidly baroque building topped by a slim tower with a chiming clock, at Christmas and Fallas it dresses up with strings of lights and the effect is stunning.
🕐 *5 min. Plaza Ayuntamiento 1.*
☎ *96-352-5478. Admission free. Daily 10am–1pm. Metro: Xàtiva.*

❹ ★★ kids Palacio de Correos y Telégrafos. This sumptuous wedding cake of a building functions as the main post office. Completed

The parrot on top of the Mercado Central.

in 1922 following a contest in 1914, it's a mix of modernism, classicism, and baroque—it shouldn't work, but somehow it pulls it off spectacularly. During a recent refurbishment, the imposing metal tower you see was reinstated after the earlier one disappeared. Inside, the circular main hall columns support a magnificent domed, stained-glass roof. Try out the whispering gallery effect here—stand by the third pillar on the right and whisper to your friend on the opposite side, who will hear you perfectly. 🕐 *20 min. Plaza Ayuntamiento.* ☎ *96-310-2730. Mon–Sat 8.30am–8.30pm. Sun 9.30am–2pm. Metro: Xàtiva.*

❺ Bar La Lonja. Just by the Mercado Central, with its hustle and bustle, La Lonja is a great place to take in the view of the market and its parrot on the roof. I love to stop awhile here for an inexpensive midmorning snack (*almuerzo*). The service is rapid and friendly. *C/ Palafox 1.* ☎ *96-351-1334. $.*

6 ★★★ **kids** Mercado Central. This vast, bustling, living market is a real glimpse of everyday Valencian life. Said to be one of the oldest market sites in Europe, it is housed in a wonderful Modernista building, completed in 1928. Having recently undergone a major refurbishment, the ceramics, ironwork, and glasswork are now a delight, and evoke scenes of the *huerta* (farmland). The market claims to be the largest area in Europe for trading fresh produce, almost 1,000 stalls sell everything from locally grown vegetables to fresh fish, seafood, and meats—the perfect place to get local delicacies. ⏱ *40 min. Plaza del Mercado s/n.* ☎ *96-382-9101. Mon–Sat 7.30am– 2.30pm. Metro: Xàtiva.*

7 ★★★ **kids** La Lonja de la Seda. This 15th-century masterpiece is one of the best examples of Gothic civil architecture in the city and was declared a UNESCO Mankind World Heritage Site in 1996. Designed and built by Pere Compte (1447–1506) as a silk exchange, the main part of the building was completed in just 15 years, an amazing feat for its time. Come here to admire the magnificent Sala de Contratación—a lofty, spacious area with beautiful helicoidal (barley twist) columns—or walk through to the cool courtyard garden filled with orange trees and verdant plants. Outside, the gargoyles are extremely rude! Best not point these out to the children. ⏱ *20 min. Plaza del Mercado s/n.* ☎ *96-352-5478. Admission free. Tues–Sat 10am–2pm & 4.30–8.30pm, Sun 10am–3pm. Metro: Xàtiva.*

8 ★ **kids** Plaza Redonda. This pretty square—built in 1840—is actually circular and has a little fountain at its center. During the week, it is home to, mainly, haberdashery and ceramics shops, but at the weekend Plaza Redonda becomes part of the market that runs through the *barrio* (neighborhood). The fainthearted may not approve of the very young puppies and kittens on sale. ⏱ *30 min. Plaza Redonda.*

9 ★ El Kiosko. This is a strictly 'no-frills' lunchtime venue and is renowned for offering an excellent value 3-course lunch (wine or beer included) or just great tapas. A

Ceiling of the 15th-century La Lonja de la Seda.

favorite of locals (myself included) and visitors alike, it is on the square behind La Lonja. On a sunny day, you can sit outside and people-watch while you dine. The interior is traditional Valencian, just like the food they serve. *C/ de los Derechos 38.* ☎ *96-391-0159. $.*

⑩ ★★★ kids **Palacio Del Marques De Dos Aguas (Museo Nacional de Ceramica Gonzalez Marti).** When you first set eyes on this edifice, you understand the meaning of the term 'breathtaking'. The baroque alabaster entrance to this unique palace—an eclectic mix of rococo, neoclassical, and Oriental architecture—is almost unbelievably ornate and over-the-top. In the 18th century, Hipolito Rovira (1693–1763) remodeled this 16th-century palace with the elaborately detailed *Churrigueresque* façade (named after the 16th-century Salamanca family who first used the style), aided by sculptor Ignacio Vergara (1715–1776). It now houses the **National Ceramics Museum,** a collection of ceramics from prehistory to the present. I particularly like the turn-of-the-century Valencian kitchen made completely from ceramics and a full-size carriage Cinderella would have been proud of. ⏲ *45 min. C/ Poeta Querol 2.* ☎ *96-351-6392. www.mnceramica. mcu.es. Admission 2€: Tues–Sat 10am–2pm & 4–8pm; Admission free: Sun 10am–2pm. Metro: Xàtiva.*

⑪ ★★★ kids **La Catedral de Valencia & El Miguelete.** Dominating the Plaza de la Reina is Valencia's cathedral. Work commenced in 1262 when they began to build over the old Central Mosque. Modification over the centuries has led to a combination of architectural styles: Romanesque, Renaissance, Gothic, baroque, and neoclassical. The cathedral's main claim to fame is

that it is supposedly home to the Holy Grail (see box p 28), a chalice taken by St. Peter to Rome and then brought by way of Huesca to Valencia during the Crusades. Pope Benedict XVI conducted Mass here during his visit in 2006. A more bizarre and grotesque treasure is the mummified severed arm of San Vicente Martír. The Cathedral's bell-tower, El Miguelete (El Micalet in Valenciano), is one of the city's iconic symbols. In the Gothic main entrance take the door to the left for the tower and climb 207 steps to the top for one of the best panoramic views of the city, across the rich fields of farmland and out to the sea. The right door gives entry to the cathedral tour (this will require more time than allocated but is worth it if only to see the mummified arm). ⏲ *30 min. Plaza de la Reina, s/n.* ☎ *96-391-8127. www.catedraldevalencia.es. Admission 3€ adults. El Miguelete ⏲ 1 hr. 2.50€ See p 27, bullet ❸ & ❹.*

⑫ ★★★ kids **La Plaza de la Virgen & Basílica de Nuestra Señora de los Desamparados.** Valencia is built over the original Roman city of Valentia (meaning 'strength and good luck') and the Plaza de la Virgen, arguably the most important square in Valencia, is where the Roman forum once was. Not only is it one of the most visited squares in the city, but it is used for all sorts of festivities, both religious and secular. At almost any time of the year you're likely to find something happening here. At the top end of the plaza is a fountain, depicting, in human form, the Río (river) Túria and its tributaries, not one of my favorite sculptures. Then, pretty orange gardens face the Basílica de Nuestra Señora de los Desamparados (Basilica of Our Lady of the Helpless), dedicated to the city's patron saint. Her nickname *la* *cheperudeta*, meaning 'the hunchback', is taken from the original Gothic sculpture, and her hair is from the heads of Falleras, the queens of Las Fallas (see p 122). The Basilica, designed by an architect from Requena, Diego Martínez Ponce de Urrana, was completed in 1667. Look up at the vaulted ceiling to see baroque paintings of the Virgin by Antonio Palomino (1653–1726). ⏱ *30 min. Plaza de la Virgen Basílica de Nuestra Señora de los Desamparados, Plaza de la Virgen. ☎ 96-391-8611. Open during services. Admission free. Metro: Xàtiva. See p 29, bullet ❻ & ❼.*

❸ ★ **kids** **Torres de Serranos.** These enormous and stunning gothic towers, built in the 14th century, were the main entrance to the Christian walled city that became home for travelers from Catalonia, Aragon, and Serranía. Although built to withstand enemy forces, they were never used in battle. The

View across the Plaza de la Virgen.

Torres have seen varied duty over the centuries, most famously as a prison for nobility and latterly, in the Spanish Civil War, as a warehouse to protect works of art. The short climb to the top offers wonderful views over the Río Túria, the city's glorious park (see p 70) and in the other direction, the city itself. ⏱ *40 min. Plaza de los Fueros s/n. ☎ 96-391-9070. Open Tues–Sun 10am–2pm & 4.30–8.30pm Sun 10am–3pm. Admission 2€. Bus: 1, 6, 8, 11, 16, 26, 29, 36, 80, 95.*

14 **La Crêpe.** A tiny bar with tables on the terraces of the Plaza de la Virgen (all year round), there's no room inside. They serve excellent crêpes, good coffee, juices, and refreshments, and with one of the best views of the plaza and the Cathedral and Basilica. *C/ Caballeros. No phone. $.*

The Best in Two Days

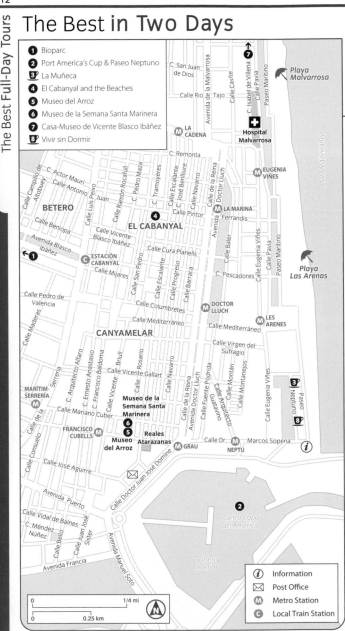

1. Bioparc
2. Port America's Cup & Paseo Neptuno
3. La Muñeca
4. El Cabanyal and the Beaches
5. Museo del Arroz
6. Museo de la Semana Santa Marinera
7. Casa-Museo de Vicente Blasco Ibáñez
8. Vivir sin Dormir

ⓘ	Information
✉	Post Office
Ⓜ	Metro Station
Ⓒ	Local Train Station

Today, I'll take you on a trip to the zoo followed by an afternoon at the port of Valencia and on to the beach—and why not? With more than 300 days of sunshine during the year, the chances are you'll want to take it easy. For the more energetic, I'll pick up the pace and introduce you to a couple of small museums. START: **For the Bioparc and Parque Cabecera take Metro to Nou D'Octubre or bus 7, 17, 29, 61, 81, or 95.**

1 ★★★ **Bioparc (Valencia's Zoo).** Even people who don't approve of zoos are giving Valencia's latest attraction a huge thumbs-up. The zoo is unique, employing what is termed 'Zoo-immersion'. The result is an accurate likeness of the animals' natural habitats, ensuring both you and the animals find it believable: there are no cages and the animals seem completely content. At the time of writing, the parks named Equatorial Africa, the Savannas, and Madagascar are open and are very impressively similar to the areas they set out to represent. In Madagascar, for example, dozens of lemurs play, walk, and leap around as you wander through their enclosure. My wife and I had a coffee in the inexpensive thatched, bush-style lakeside cafeteria and restaurant while giraffe and antelope came to drink at the water's edge almost within our reach. It is idyllic; so do visit for

refreshments before you leave. ⏱ *3 hr. Avenida Pío Baroja, 3. www.bioparcvalencia.es. Admission 20€ adults, 15€ children. Daily 10am–8pm. Metro: Nou D'Octubre. Bus: 7, 17, 29, 61, 81, 95.*

2 ★★ **kids Port America's Cup & Paseo Neptuno.** Valencia is frequently described as the city that turned its back on the sea. Some say that it's only in the past few years, with the advent of the America's Cup (the world's most prestigious sailing race and regatta), that it has remembered the sea is there. The decaying port was refurbished to make Port America's Cup and had new team 'Houses' and the marvelous *Veles e Vents* (Sails and Winds) building, designed by UK architect David Chipperfield, constructed for the international event in 2007. It is now better than ever with part of the Formula One street circuit passing around the port. Just

Veles e Vents in the Marina.

Malvarrosa, Valencia's enormous beach.

next to the port is **Paseo Neptuno,** a line of excellent restaurants and bars along the promenade serving, in the main, traditional Valencian fare—especially the ubiquitous paella. A quick perusal of menus outside each establishment will soon tell you that they all offer the same—mainly rice dishes and fish. The majority of restaurants here are excellent, but the most famous, reflected in its size and prices, is La Pepica, where Hemingway famously ate. ⏲ *2 hr. Port America's Cup and Paseo Neptuno. Metro: Neptú.*

3 **La Muñeca.** La Muñeca is one of my favorites among the many restaurants on Paseo Neptuno. They offer a wide variety of rice dishes and a huge selection of market fresh fish. Busy most days of the week, it is particularly so on Sundays, when it fills with large, loud Valencian family lunches. It's advisable to book ahead. The Terraza has lovely views to the beach. *Paseo Neptuno 64.* ☎ *96-371-2083. $$.*

4 **El Cabanyal and the Beaches.** The city beaches from Malvarrosa in Barrio El Cabanyal, just by the port, through to the barrio of Patacona are wide and sandy, and all have the coveted blue flags, meaning they are beautifully clean and safe. Showers and toilets are found at regular intervals along the beach,

and sun-loungers and umbrellas are available for hire, too. There are various play areas, nets for beach volleyball, and other games. Red Cross lifeguards patrol the beaches and the sea during the summer, and there is plenty of parking right next to the promenade. Most weekends, street traders ply their wares along the prom selling souvenirs, clothes, and jewelry. ⏲ *30 min. Tram: Dr Lluch. Metro: Neptú.*

5 **Museo del Arroz.** El Cabanyal, one of several barrios (districts) that make up the port area, is closest to the sea. The old fishing village was getting a little frayed round the edges but is now part of elaborate plans for a new seaside resort. Rice is a major ingredient in the region's cooking, and the Museo del Arroz (Rice Museum) is almost the first building you come to on Calle del Rosario. Inside this restored rice mill from the early 1900s, you can see how rice was processed at the turn of the last century. ⏲ *15 min. C/ Rosario 1, Cabanyal.* ☎ *96-367-6291. www.museoarrozvalencia.com. Admission 2€ adults & 1€ children, students, & senior citizens. Open Tues–Sat 10am–2pm & 4.30–8.30pm, Sun/hols 10am–3pm. Metro: Neptú.*

6 **Museo de la Semana Santa Marinera (Maritime Holy Week Museum).** The seaside *barrio* of El Cabanyal is famous for its annual, solemn Easter Celebrations;

Semana Santa Marinera (see p 155) is almost as legendary in Spain as the similar celebrations in Seville. The week-long festivities involve brotherhoods of sinister-looking penitents who parade through the streets in pointed hoods and capes. The museum is devoted to the traditions of this Holy Week and has photos and costumes; it is in the same building as the Rice Museum (see bullet ❺). ⏱ *30 min. C/ Rosario 1, Cabanyal.* ☎ *96-324-0745. www. semanasantamarinera.org. Admission 2€ adults & 1€ children, students, & senior citizens. Open Tues–Sat 10am–2pm & 4.30–8.30pm, Sun/hols 10am–3pm. Metro: Neptú.*

❼ **Casa-Museo de Vicente Blasco Ibáñez (House-Museum of Vicente Blasco Ibáñez).** At the other end of Malvarrosa beach is the House of Vicente Blasco Ibáñez (1867–1928), Valencia's most internationally famous writer. His best-known work is *The Four Horsemen of the Apocalypse*, which Hollywood has filmed four times over the years. It is in this house that Ibáñez wrote his famous novel, sitting at a huge stone desk on the terrace overlooking the sea. Lucky man! ⏱ *30 min.*

Casa-Museo de Vicente Blasco Ibáñez.

C/ Isabel de Villena 157. ☎ *96-352-5478. Tues–Sat 10am–2pm & 4.30–8pm. Sun 10am–3pm. Tram: Dr Lluch.*

🍵 ★ **Vivir sin Dormir (Live without Sleep).** A great Valencian haunt and a key part of the famous 'bacalao' (see p 106) in the '70s. It has 'hung on in there', as they say, and is still a very pleasant place to have a few drinks after an afternoon at the beach. *Paseo Neptuno 42–44.* ☎ *93-418-5879. $.*

La Semana Santa Marinera.

The Best in Three Days

Calle Llano de la Zaidia

Calle Mauro Guillem

Calle Manyá

Calle Sagunto

Calle Pintor Vilar

Calle Almazora

Calle Cronista Rivelles

Calle Alborava

Puente
San José

Jardines
del Turia

PONT DE
FUSTA

Puente de
las Artes

Casa Museo
Benlliure ❺

C. Guillem de
Castro

C. Salvador
Giner

C. Na Jordana

Calle Blanquerías

Real Monasterio
de la Trinidad

IVAM ❹

Iglesia del
Carmen

Puente de
Serranos

Calle Cronista Rivelles

Museo de
Bellas Artes

❸ Centro Cultural
la Beneficencia

Plaza
Carmen

Torres de
Serranos ❻

Plaza
Fueros ❼

Puente
Trinidad

Calle San Pío V

Calle Corona

Calle Alta

Plaza
Cisneros

Calle Pintor López

C. Dr. Beltrán Bigorra

C. Baja

Calle Serranos

C. Portal
d. Valldigna

LA SEU

Basílica de Nuestra
Señora de los
Desamparados

C. Trinitarios

Plaza
del Temple

Calle Guillem de Castro

EL CARMEN

Plaza
Tossal

Calle Caballeros

San
Nicolás

Plaza de
la Virgen

Almudín

Museo de
la Ciudad

❷ Torres
de Quart

Calle Quart

Calle Murillo

C. Bolsería

Catedral

San Vicente
Mártir

LA
XEREA

C. Pintor Domingo

La
Lonja

Santa
Catalina

Plaza
de la
Reina

Plaza
Tetuán

Santos Tomás y
San Felipe Neri

Santos
Juanes

Calle del Mar

Calle Carniceros

Plaza Don
Juan de
Vilarrasa

Calle de la Paz

Calle Balmes

Mercado
Central

Av. María Cristina

Museo de
Cerámica

El Patriarca

Calle Camarón

C. Moratín

Calle Bany

EL PILAR

Avenida Barón de Cárcer

Calle Músico Peydró

Calle San Vicente Mártir

Plaza R.
Botet

Universidad
de Valencia

C. Poeta Querol

Plaza Alfonso
El Magnánimo

Sorolla

Calle Hospital

Iglesia
del Pilar

MUVIM ❶

Calle Quevedo

Plaza
Ayuntamiento

Calle Barcas

C. Poeta
Quintana

Calle Pintor

C. Don Juan de Austria

COLÓN

Calle Guillem de Castro

C. María Jacer

Ayuntamiento

Calle Correos

Calle Sagasta

de Lauria

EL PLA
DEL REMEI

Gran Vía de
Ramón y Cajal

San
Agustín

Avenida
Marqués de Sotelo

Calle Jesús

Calle Xàtiva

Calle Ribera

Calle Roger

Paseo Ruzafa

Calle Pascual y Genís

Calle de Colón

Calle Picarro

C. Cirilo Amorós

XÁTIVA

Estación
del Norte

Plaza de
Toros

Calle Ruzafa

Calle Félix Pizcueta

C. Martí

Calle Castellón

❶ Museo de la Ilustración y
la Modernidad (MUVIM)

❷ Las Torres de Quart

❸ Centro Cultural la Beneficencia

❹ Instituto Valenciano de
Arte Moderno (IVAM)

❺ Casa-Museo José Benlliure

❻ Casa de las Rocas

❼ Casa Mario

❽ Ciudad de las Artes y las Ciencias

❾ On The Rocks

ℹ️	Information
✉️	Post Office
Ⓜ️	Metro Station

BAILÉN

0 — 1/4 mi
0 — 0.25 km

N

I've created this tour with a more leisurely pace in mind. Make a start in the morning and stroll around the city and along the river park, Río Túria, taking in a few museums. Begin at one of the city's newest, MUVIM, and walk, by way of La Beneficencia to IVAM, Valencia's Contemporary Art Museum, rated one of the finest in Europe. To finish the morning, check out the extraordinary Corpus Christi floats housed in a unique museum near the Torres de Serranos. After lunch, grab a bus to the fantastic and futuristic Ciudad de las Artes y las Ciencias (City of Arts and Sciences) and the Oceanogràfic. START: Bus 5 or 11 to Guillém de Castro or metro to Angel Guiméra.

① ★★ kids Museo de la Ilustración y la Modernidad (MUVIM). The Museum of Enlightenment and Modernity has one of the most wonderful names for a museum I've come across, though the name in fact actually refers to a permanent audiovisual presentation based on thought, from the European Age of Enlightenment of the 18th century to the present day. If you want to see this beautifully made presentation, you have to book. This is best done the day before—ask the hotel to phone for you. The presentation takes an hour and is visually and aurally stunning. There are usually excellent temporary exhibits as well as a pleasant gallery shop and café. ⏱ *1hr 20 min. Guillém de Castro 8.* ☎ *96-388-3730. www.muvim.es. Admission free. Tues–Sat 10am–2pm & 4–8pm, Sun 10am–8pm; year-round. Metro: Angel Guiméra.*

② ★ kids Las Torres de Quart. Once one of the gates to the medieval walled city of Valencia, these towers were used as a women's prison from 1626 until well into the 18th century. They have withstood battles and sieges, and even the demolition of the city walls in the 19th century (this tower and the Serranos towers are virtually all that remain). They still bear the scars from the siege of the city by Napoleon's troops in 1808. There

was great consternation from some quarters when the city fathers decided on a restoration project for these towers: some people thought the holes and marks would be 'restored away'. They need not have worried though, as the towers are still battle-worn and cannon-marked. Like the Torres de Serranos you saw on the first day (see bullet **⑬**, p 11), these too can be scaled for views of this part of the city. ⏱ *40 min. Guillém de Castro 89. Admission free. Tues–Sun 10am–2pm & 4–8pm. Metro: Angel Guiméra.*

③ ★★ kids Centro Cultural la Beneficencia. This wonderful building, recently completely restored, houses two museums: the

Cannonball damage on the walls of the Torres de Quart.

Courtyard of La Beneficencia.

Museum of Prehistory and the **Valencian Ethnology Museum.** It is a charming place to visit, not least for its beautiful blue-and-white tiled central courtyard. The coffee shop here is worth a visit—take a seat and absorb the atmosphere while imbibing a well-earned refreshment. ⏱ *1 hr. C/ Corona 36.* ☎ *96-388-3665. Admission free. Tues–Sun 10am–8pm. Metro: Angel Guiméra.*

❹ ★★ **Instituto Valenciano de Arte Moderno (IVAM).** Opened in 1989, IVAM was Spain's first modern art museum and is now considered one of the country's—and

maybe the world's—finest contemporary art spaces. It comprises seven galleries, including one of the world's largest permanent collections of the work of cubist and abstract painter and sculptor Julio González (1876–1942). The museum has a fine international program of the best painters and sculptors in the world and is well worth a visit at any time of the year. I find watching the visitors looking at contemporary art can be as rewarding as the art itself. ⏱ *1 hr. Guillém de Castro 118.* ☎ *96-388-9000. www.ivam.es. Admission 2.10€. Admission free Sun. June–Sep Tues–Sun 10am–10pm. Oct–May Tues–Sun 10am–8pm. Metro: Túria.*

❺ ★★ **Casa-Museo José Benlliure.** I think this is a gem of a museum, and is a little bit of a secret. It is the house of 19th-century painter José Benlliure, (1855–1937) one of Valencia's favorite sons and a contemporary of the internationally famous Joaquín Sorolla (1863–1923). The ground floor is his house as he would have lived in it and out the back is a beautiful secluded garden, which is gloriously cool and shady in the height of summer. It is tempting not to tell you about the wonderful surprise on

Steps of the Modern Art Museum, IVAM.

An ancient float or rocas.

the first floor of the building at the back of the garden, but this is a guidebook, after all. At the top of the stairs, you'll find a small wooden door: enter to step inside José's studio. If you're anything like me, you'll definitely get a tingling feeling—it's as if Benlliure has just stepped out the room and will be back at any moment. An Aladdin's cave of objects, it is filled with personal effects, books, ceramics, Victoriana, and paintings. A rare delight.
🕐 *45 min. C/ Blanquerias 23.*
☎ *96-391-1662. Admission 2 €.*
Admission free on Sun. Tues–Sun 10am–2pm & 4.30pm to 8.30pm. Metro: Túria.

⑥ ★ kids Casa de las Rocas.
Each year at Corpus Christi (60 days after Easter) a procession of highly ornate floats depicting biblical scenes and morality tales makes its way from this museum to the Plaza de la Virgen (see p 10, bullet ⑫). These processions are famous throughout Spain and have taken place since 1326. This Gothic building was built as a 'garage' for *las rocas* or floats, in the 15th century, and is now a small museum that houses not just the floats but images

and costumes. When I first visited some years ago it was dark and fore-boding inside, and a wizened old couple would put dim lights on as you walked around the exhibits. It is now a well-organized museum. The wooden rocas are ancient—one dates back to the 16th century—but the most ornate are from the 18th. '*Faith*' is one of the oldest, built in 1560, the title illustrated by a beautifully carved wooden blind-folded figure. There are also giant caricature figures that are worn on strong shoulders during the proces-sions. 🕐 *30 min. C/ Las Rocas 3.*
☎ *96-315-3156. Admission 2€. Mon–Fri 10am–2pm. Metro: Túria.*

⑦ ★ Casa Mario. A little bar with tables on the street all year round, it faces the Torres de Serranos and serves delicious tapas and fresh fish. Their menu is essentially a traditional lunch menu but there are little twists to the dishes. Inside is small and intimate and the service is friendly.
C/ Roteros 3. ☎ *96-392-4452. $.*

⑧ ★★★ kids Ciudad de las Artes y las Ciencias. The

The Science Museum at the Ciudad de las Artes y las Ciencias.

stunning futuristic architecture of Santiago Calatrava and Felix Candela converted this ugly bit of marshland in the Río Túria into one of the best-known leisure parks in the world, attracting around 5 million visitors a year and making it the second most visited attraction in Spain (beaten to the post by Madrid's Museo del Prado). The 'City of Arts and Sciences' consists of five separate areas: the Palau de les Arts is a multifunctional arts center; Museo de las Ciencias Principe Felipe, a science museum; L'Hemisfèric, an Imax cinema; then there's L'Umbracle, housing aromatic gardens and providing a wonderful view of the complex; and lastly, the Oceanogràfic, which, in my view, is the highlight of all five. It has the largest aquarium in Europe, with a dolphin show that visitors say can rival any in the world. Although it is a great place to visit on any day, I think it's particularly perfect when the weather is really hot, because most of the aquarium is below ground. There are several 'oceans' to visit, from Polar to Mediterranean, and schools of fish—including sharks and giant rays—swim around you in the two glass tunnels, one more than 70m/230ft long. The dolphin show (included in ticket price) changes time depending on the season, so check on arrival. 🕐 *4 hr minimum. Avenida Autopista del Saler, 1–7.* ☎ *90-210-0031. Oceanogràfic. Admission 22.80 € adults, 17.20€ children. Daily 10am–2pm. Metro: Túria. See p 25, bullet* ❼. *See also Chapter 2: I Have Seen the Future.*

☕ ★★ **On The Rocks.** What better way to round off a day at the City of Arts and Sciences than in a cool (in every sense of the word) bar, watching the sunset on the marvels of the ciudad's modern architecture? This chillout bar is all white walls and sleek furniture, and opens daily from 10am to 3.30am uninterrupted, playing the smoothest sounds and serving the coolest drinks. *Paseo de la Alameda 45.* ☎ *96-381-4330. www.valenciaontherocks.com. $$.* ●

I Have Seen the Future—The City of Arts & Sciences

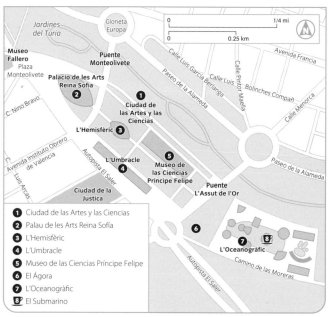

1. Ciudad de las Artes y las Ciencias
2. Palau de les Arts Reina Sofía
3. L'Hemisfèric
4. L'Umbracle
5. Museo de las Ciencias Príncipe Felipe
6. El Ágora
7. L'Oceanogràfic
8. El Submarino

L a Ciudad de las Artes y las Ciencias is thought by many to be the key reason for Valencia's growth and success as a tourist destination over the past few years. It is certainly true if you look at the number of visitors it receives annually: around five million people passed through the complex last year. The main architect of this stunningly futuristic 'city' is internationally famous Valencian-born Santiago Calatrava. Work is still in progress with more buildings including three enormous tower blocks, the tallest in Spain, planned for construction in future years. START: **From the city center take buses 95, 35, 19, or 40. Or a half-an-hour walk along the riverbed.**

❶ ★★★ kids **Ciudad de las Artes y las Ciencias.** The 'City of Arts and Sciences' is now one of the best-known and most photographed leisure parks in the world. Consisting of 350,000 sq m/86.5 acres of 'intelligent entertainment', the park is a stunning example of modern architecture. It is divided into six main areas: the Palau de les Arts, L'Hemisfèric, L'Umbracle, Museo de las Ciencias Principe Felipe, L'Assut de l'Or, El Ágora, and L'Oceanogràfic. All are surrounded by public walkways, water-filled pools, and over 7,000 sq m/75,300 sq ft of

L'Hemisfèric.

green space. The outside space is used to great effect each year for the free Festival Eclèctic that is held every July. Street theater and music, juggling and spectacular concerts all take place in and around the buildings, and stages are erected over the pools for concerts, both pop and classical. With such a marvelous setting, Diana, my wife, and I always make sure we are in town for an enjoyable few days of entertainment under the moon of Valencia. ⏲ *At least two full days. Avinguda Autopista del Saler.* ☎ *90-210-0031. www.cac.es. Admission from 30.60€ adults, 23.30€ concessions and children (4–12), free under 3s. Daily 10am–9pm (high season), 10am–7pm (low season). (L'Oceanogràfic has different opening times. See p 25, bullet* ❼*) Bus: 19, 35, 40, 95.*

❷ ★★★ **kids** **Palau de les Arts Reina Sofía.** Valencia's opera house seats 2,500 in its multi-functional auditorium, which boasts state-of-the-art technology throughout. There are also four smaller halls, designed and dedicated to the performing arts. 'Opera Season' begins in October each year, and

most performances sell out within hours of tickets going on sale. The building is stunning, a huge shiny egg against the sky, and every time I pass it I stand amazed at the flying canopy that seems to hover above the main structure. Even more astounding is how delicate the base and support of the canopy look. ⏲ *15 min. See p 22, bullet* ❶.

❸ ★★★ **kids** **L'Hemisfèric.** Home to a 180-degree Planetarium, Laserium, and an IMAX cinema, this building was cleverly designed to look like an eye—most genius is the glass-and-metal outer shell that opens and closes like an eyelid from time to time. Throughout the year, there is a noteworthy timetable of films, all of which have commentaries or soundtracks in various languages that you can listen to through headphones. A word of warning if you are prone to motion sickness, this is a 180° surround cinema and some scenes can certainly make you feel a little woozy (see p 19). ⏲ *1 hr. www.cac.es. Admission free as part of CAC ticket, otherwise 7.50€. Daily shows every hour throughout the day.*

The Umbracle at the Ciudad de las Artes y Ciencias.

④ ★★★ **kids** **L'Umbracle.** Standing at 60m/195ft high, this palm tree-filled, skeletal structure serves as a pedestrian entrance to the 'city'. A large and attractive variety of aromatic plants from around the world fill the garden terrace, and, here and there, sculptures, including one by Yoko Ono, add to the interest. The terrace offers incredible views over the whole City of Arts and Sciences. Underneath are a car park and a discotheque (M.Y.A.). The large white sparkly cones at each end house elevators to the car parks and lower floors. During the summer months, part of the terrace is sectioned off for use as an open-air nightclub and chill-out area, which goes by the same name as the structure—L'Umbracle. (See p 111.) ⏱ *30 min. www.cac.es. Admission to the terrace is free at all times. Nightclub admission prices vary from night to night. www. umbracleterraza.com.*

⑤ ★★★ **kids** **Museo de las Ciencias Príncipe Felipe.** The biggest of the buildings in the 'city', this enormous white mosaic and glass building is Valencia's science museum. Different sections cover all areas of science from electricity, light and sound, to how the body works. Our younger nieces and nephews always enjoy the section on sport where they test their ability in speed, strength, balance, and agility. Downstairs there are cafeterias and a shop, where you can purchase some well-designed souvenirs at very reasonable prices. ⏱ *3–4 hr or more. See p 22, bullet* ①.

⑥ ★★★ **kids** **El Ágora.** The latest addition to the 'city', along with the L'Assut de l'Or, a huge suspension bridge that will link the newer barrios of Valencia, is the Ágora, which is being built primarily as a home for the Spanish Open Tennis. These soaring and space age new structures are, once again, both the work of Santiago Calatrava. The 70m/230ft tall Ágora will seat 5,000 people in its main space—it will become Valencia's biggest auditorium and will also be used for other major public events and concerts in the city. ⏱ *45 min. See p 72.*

7 ★★★ **kids** **L'Oceanogràfic.** Europe's largest aquarium is worth setting aside a full day for. It was designed by Spanish-American architect Félix Candela, who died before he could see it completed. Much of it is underground and air-conditioned—so it's perfect for all the family to visit, even in high summer. The futuristic buildings are set around the central lake. The aquarium is split into eight different areas covering the Arctic, Antarctic, Mediterranean, Oceans, Tropical and Temperate, Islands, Wetlands, and a conservation area dedicated to two of the most threatened animal groups of the Mediterranean coast, turtles and dolphins. 45,000 animals from more than 50 species co-exist. My favorite part has to be the 70m/230ft glass tunnel where rare species swim all around you as you wander through. The Dolphinarium seats 2,210 people and whenever I have been, both the dolphins and their trainers genuinely seem to be enjoying themselves. If you're in the city in high summer, try to catch the special, late-night synchronized swimming and dolphin show. ⏲ *A full day. www.cac.es. Admission free as part of a CAC ticket, otherwise 23.30€ adult, 17.60€ concessions and children (4–12), free under 3s. Daily 10am–midnight (high season); 10am–8pm (mid-season); 10am–6pm Sun–Fri & 10am–8pm Sat (low season).Check on arrival for dolphin show times.*

8 ★★ **El Submarino.** This restaurant is one of the first buildings you see as you enter L'Oceanogràfic. An interesting menu served in unique surroundings— all around you fish swim behind glass. Reservations are essential as this is a proper dining experience. *Paletilla de cordero lechal* (shoulder of baby lamb) is one of my favorite dishes and is perfect here. Elsewhere in the complex are reasonably priced family restaurants and cafés if you fancy a quick bite. *L'Oceanogràfic.* ☎ *96-197-5565. $$–$$$. Open daily 1.30–4pm & 8.30–11.30pm. Closed Sun evening.*

Dolphins at L'Oceanogràfic.

Centro Histórico: Ancient Valencia

1. Horchatería Santa Catalina
2. Plaza de la Reina
3. La Catedral
4. El Miguelete
5. Pepe Pepica
6. Plaza de la Virgen
7. Basílica de Nuestra Señora de los Desamparados
8. Plaza de la Almoina
9. Cripta de la Cárcel de San Vicente Mártir

ⓘ Information
✉ Post Office
Ⓜ Metro Station

0		1/4 mi
0	0.25 km	

At the heart of Valencia is its cathedral, basilica, and the ruins of the Roman city of Valentia. The Romans first arrived in 138 B.C. with a modest settlement of soldiers. During the next few years, Valentia suffered various ups and downs, and by the year 300 A.D fell into decay. The Moors were the next major influence on the city and by the 10th century, the city was the capital of the Moorish Kingdom. The Moors were responsible for the introduction of the silk trade and planted rice and oranges. El Cid then ousted the Arabs towards the end of the 11th century, and in 1238 A.D. Jaime (James) I conquered the city and made it the capital of the new Kingdom of Valencia. START: **Buses 4, 6, 8, 9, 11, 16, 28, 36, 70, or 71 to Plaza de la Reina.**

1 **Horchatería Santa Catalina.** The sign over the door of this bar says that the 'house' has 200 years of tradition—it is certainly one of the best places to try *horchata*, a drink made from the tubers grown and known locally as *chufa* (tiger nuts in English). Order a glass, icy cold, with a couple of *fartons* (yes, you read that right!), sticky finger-buns to dunk. Delicious and so refreshing. *Plaza Santa Catalina, 6.* ☎ *96-391-2379. $.*

2 ★★★ kids **Plaza de la Reina.** This attractive cathedral square is always bustling with people, locals and tourists alike, taking coffee or a meal in one of the pavement cafés,

catching a bus, strolling to the cathedral, or just sitting on one of the tree-shaded benches in the garden watching the world go by. In front of the cathedral you can find one of several bronze models scattered throughout the city of the buildings that make up this holy part of the city; all have descriptions in Braille too, so that those who can't see the beauty of the buildings can at least feel their shape. Horses and traps await a fare and you can take one from here for a tour of the old town. ⏱ *45 min. Bus: 4, 5b, 6, 8, 9, 11, 16, 28, 36, 70, 71.*

3 ★★★ **La Catedral.** At the top of the Plaza de la Reina stands Valencia's imposing cathedral. It was built between 1252 and 1482 and

Plaza de la Reina.

The belltower of the cathedral, El Miguelete.

small museum containing many more paintings, statues, and artifacts. ⏲ *1 hr. Plaza de la Reina. www.catedraldevalencia.es. Admission from 3€, free on Sun. Mar 20–Oct 31: Mon–Sat 10am–6.30pm, Sun & hols 2–6.30pm; Nov 1–Mar 19: Mon–Sat 10am–5.30pm, Sun & hols closed 2– 5pm. Audio guides available. Book guided visits on ☎ 66-190-9687. An area is always open for prayer. Bus: 4, 5b, 6, 8, 9, 11, 16, 28, 36, 70, 71. See p 10, bullet* ⓫.

was dedicated to the Blessed Virgin by King Jaime I (Jaume in Valenciano). The cathedral is a spectacular mix of architectural styles, from neoclassical to Gothic, right up to the magnificent baroque façade of the main entrance, which was added in the early 18th century. As well as the Holy Grail (see box below), other religious and artistic treasures include two magnificent Goya paintings, a 14th-century lantern, and its most curious and gruesome relic—the mummified left arm of San Vicente Mártir, who was martyred in the city around 304 A.D. Some wonderfully preserved renaissance frescos were recently rediscovered when a nesting pigeon made a hole in the cathedral roof above the altar. These are now on display, and there is also a

❹ ★★★ 🄺🄸🄳🅂 **El Miguelete.** Something of a Valencian landmark, the clock tower El Micalet (in Valenciano) is named after Miguel (Michael), one of its bells, which chime every quarter of an hour. Take the door to the left inside the cathedral entrance for the tower. The octagonal tower stands over 51m/167ft tall, and the climb of its 207 spiral stairs is a must for the energetic. The wonderful 360-degree views of the city and El Miguelete's 'wife'—the nearby tower of Santa Catalina—more than compensate for the hike. ⏲ *45 min. Bus: 4, 5b, 6, 8, 9, 11, 16, 28, 36, 70, 71.*

❺ **Pepe Pepica.** Considering this restaurant/bar is right on the main tourist square, the food is remarkably good. What is more, it is good value, too. A set three-course lunch with paella or another rice dish as

The Holy Grail

Forget everything you have read in Dan Brown's Da Vinci Code, because the cathedral is home to what is said to be the real Holy Grail, the chalice that Christ is said to have used at the Last Supper. Made of agate and gold, and hidden in a monastery in Aragon through the dark ages, it has been in the cathedral since the 15th century and you can see it in the dark stone chapel.

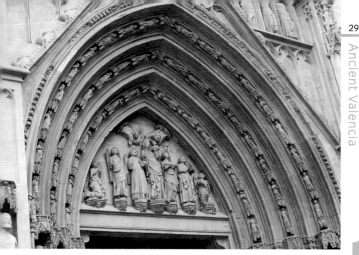

Doorway of the Cathedral facing the Plaza de la Virgen.

a starter comes in around 12€. You should find friendly and helpful service here and modern, attractive surroundings. I recommended this place to a well-traveled American tourist recently and he declared it one of the best eateries he'd ever visited—high accolade indeed. *Plaza de la Reina, 12–14.* ☎ *93-268-2598. $$.*

6 ★★★ **kids** Plaza de la Virgen. The shady marble pedestrian walkway around the outside of the cathedral brings you out into this glorious plaza, once the site of the forum in Roman Valentia. This is probably the busiest plaza in the city, both day and night, and even more so in the summer. People congregate on the steps and at the cafés around the square.

In the hottest months, it becomes the main meeting point in the early hours for residents (and visitors) to escape the heat of their homes. In winter, a stage is set up every Sunday morning for Valencian folk dancing. At the top end, the fountain of a reclining man surrounded by eight nymphs represents the River Túria and its main irrigation channels. The square is named after the Virgin Mary, and if you're to be here during Fallas (see p 122), you can watch as up to 150,000 people, dressed in traditional costume, offer flowers and floral tributes to a Virgin Mary as tall as the Basilica itself. On the second Sunday in May, the statue of the Virgin, Our Lady of the Helpless, makes a journey from the basilica to the cathedral, surrounded by a large, surging crowd who pass small children (and adults)

Bronze model of the Cathedral.

Braille description of the Cathedral in Plaza de la Almoina.

over each other's heads to touch and kiss the gilt figure's robes. 🕐 *30 min. Bus: 4, 5b, 6, 8, 9, 11, 16, 28, 36, 70, 71. See p 3, bullet* **1**.

7 ★★★ **kids Basílica de Nuestra Señora de los Desamparados.** Dedicated to Our Lady of the Helpless, the Patron Saint of Valencia, this small, oval church, completed in 1667, often struggles to cope with the sheer number of worshippers who attend its services. The ornate gilt statue of the Virgin, nicknamed *la cheperudeta* meaning 'the hunchback' (she was originally

built to lie down with a pillow beneath her head), hangs above the altar, and there is a beautifully painted domed ceiling by Antonio Palomino (1653–1726). The Basílica is a favorite place for weddings and christenings. Some weekends a seemingly never-ending queue of wedding parties enter and then leave to have their pictures taken in the plaza, all accompanied by the sound of firecrackers. I like to sit on one of the terraces in front of the Basílica to watch it all happening. 🕐 *30 min. Plaza de la Virgen.* ☎ *96-398-8611. Free admission.*

Valencia for the Blind

Around the historic center you will come across large bronze models of the churches and cathedral, with full descriptions in Braille alongside, so blind people may feel the architecture and read the text. These models are quite beautiful and are currently located in the following locations: Plaza de la Reina (see p 27, bullet 2) in front of the Cathedral, Plaza Almoina behind the cathedral, behind La Lonja in Plaza Compañia and by the Torres de Serrano (see p 11, bullet **13**). More may follow, but along with the Museu Obert (see p 160) it gives the opportunity of getting much more information at each monument (see The Savvy Traveler p 153).

Water Tribunal

Things are always happening in the Plaza de la Virgen: the ancient Water Tribunal, for instance, takes place every Thursday at noon in the door of the Cathedral. Fascinating, because it is probably the oldest democratic institution in Europe—a court meets to sort irrigation disputes and has done so for almost a millennium. It is swift, taking only around five minutes, even when there are (rare) disputes. When there are none it is over in seconds.

Open during services. Bus: 4, 5b, 6, 8, 9, 11, 16, 28, 36, 70, 71. See p 10, bullet ⓬.

❽ ★★★ kids Plaza de la Almoina. Just behind the Basilica is this quiet plaza with a very curious and original center. A shallow pool of water covers 300 sq m/3200 sq ft of glass, below which you can see the Roman ruins of Valencia. Walk around the perimeter and look down through the water and then take the door at one end to descend into one of the city's newest museums, L'Almoina with ruins from the Roman, Visigoth, and Moorish periods. The plaza also leads to the Plaza Palau, and the palace of the Archbishop of Valencia. While an attractive building, only the pointed arches remain from the 13th century. Continuous pillaging and more than one fire made it necessary to rebuild it as late as the 20th century. It is not open to the public, but a peek through the main doors will give you a view of the beautiful courtyard. Across the road is the 15th-century L'Almudin, once the city's granary, now a museum and art gallery. Whatever the exhibition, you can always see the wall paintings high up on the walls, said to record the harvests of the time. ⏱ *30 min. L'Almoina Museum* ☎ *96-208-4173. Tues–Sat 10am– 2pm & 4.30–8.30pm, Sun 10am– 3pm. Admission 2€, free on Sat, Sun and hols. Bus: 4, 5b, 6, 8, 9, 11, 16, 28, 36, 70, 71.*

❾ ★ Cripta de la Cárcel de San Vicente Mártir. If you have already seen his mummified arm in Valencia Cathedral (see bullet ❸, p 27), you may now want to see this crypt, reputed to be where the martyr San Vicente was incarcerated. It is worth visiting for the excellent 25-minute multimedia show of the life of the saint (and his very nasty death and dismemberment) and the city's history from Roman times through the Visigoths, Muslims, and The Middle Ages. Not for the squeamish! You must reserve by phone or in person at the address below—don't forget to ask for it in English. ⏱ *30 min. Plaza del Arzo-bispo 3.* ☎ *96-394-1417. Admission 2€. Tues–Sat 10am–2pm & 4.30–8pm; multimedia show at 10am, 11.30am, 1pm, 6pm & 7pm. Sun 9.30am–2pm; multimedia show at 10.30am, 11.30am, 12.30pm & 1.30pm. Bus: 4, 5b, 6, 8, 9, 11, 16, 28, 36, 70, 71.*

Valencia for Kids

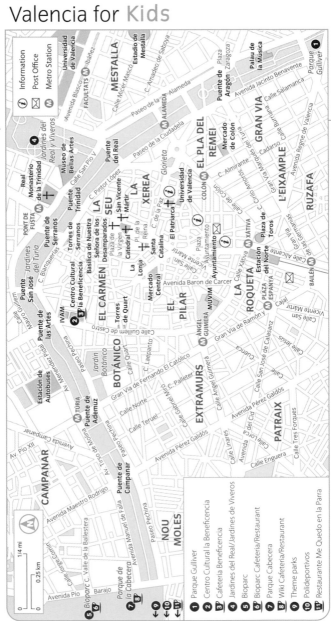

Legend:
- ⓘ Information
- ⊠ Post Office
- Ⓜ Metro Station

Map labels:
MESTALLA · Universidad de Valencia · Estadio de Mestalla · FACULTATS · Ⓜ Ibáñez · Calle Micer Mascó · C. Amadeo de Saboya · Avenida Blasco · Paseo de la Alameda · Ⓜ ALAMEDA · Puente de Aragón · Plaza Zaragoza · Palau de la Música · Avenida Jacinto Benavente · Calle Salamanca · Parque Gulliver ❶ · GRAN VIA · Mercado de Colón · C. Almirante Cadarso · Avenida Regne de Valencia · EL PLA DEL REMEI · L'EIXAMPLE · RUZAFA · COLON Ⓜ · Calle de Colón · Gran Vía Marqués del Turia · Avenida Regne de Valencia · Real Monasterio de la Trinidad · Jardines del Real y Viveros ❹ · Museo de Bellas Artes · Puente del Real · Paseo de la Ciudadela · Glorieta · Universidad de Valencia · El Patriarca · Jardines del Real · PONT DE FUSTA Ⓜ · Puente de Trinidad · C. Pintor López · LA SEU · LA XEREA · San Vicente Martir · C. de la Paz · Plaza de la Reina · XÀTIVA Ⓜ · Plaza de Toros · Estación del Norte · Gran Vía Germanías · BAILEN · Calle Alicante · Calle San Vicente Martir · Torres de Serranos · Basílica de Nuestra Señora de los Desamparados · Plaza de la Virgen · Catedral · Santa Catalina · La Lonja · Mercado Central · Ayuntamiento · Plaza Ayuntamiento · Avenida Barón de Carcer · EL CARMEN · EL PILAR · Centro Cultural la Beneficencia ❷❸ · IVAM · Torres de Quart · Calle Guillem de Castro · MUVIM · LA ROQUETA · PLAZA ESPANYA Ⓜ · Cajal · ANGEL GUIMERA Ⓜ · Gran Vía de Ramón y Cajal · Calle Jesús · Calle San Vicente Martir · Puente San José · Jardines del Turia · C. Blanquerías · Puente de Serranos · Calle Guillem · Mauro · Av. Menéndez Pidal · Paseo Pechina · Puente de las Artes · Jardín Botánico · BOTÁNICO · Calle Quart · Gran Vía de Fernando El Católico · Calle Cuenca · Calle Angel Guimerá · Calle San José de Calasanz · EXTRAMURS · Calle Norte · Calle Gabriel Miró · C. Palleter · Calle Teruel · Avenida Pérez Galdós · Calle Linares · Avenida del Cid · Calle Lorca · Avenida Pérez Galdós · PATRAIX · Calle Tres Forques · Calle Enguera · Estación de Autobuses · TURIA Ⓜ · Puente de Ademuz · Av. Pío XII · Avenida Campanar · CAMPANAR · Avenida Maestro Rodrigo · Av. Tirso de Molina · Puente de Campanar · Paseo Pechina · Avenida Manuel de Falla · Parque de la Cabecera · NOU MOLES · Avenida Pío · Barajo · Bioparc ❺❻ · Calle C. Valle de la Ballestera · Calle José Mª Haro Común

Scale:
0 — 1/4 mi
0 — 0.25 km

Numbered list:
❶ Parque Gulliver
❷ Centro Cultural la Beneficencia
❸ Cafetería Beneficencia
❹ Jardines del Real/Jardines de Viveros
❺ Bioparc
❻ Bioparc Cafetería/Restaurant
❼ Parque Cabecera
❽ Wiki Cafetería/Restaurant
❾ Theme parks
❿ Polideportivos
⓫ Restaurante Me Quedo en la Parra

Valencia is a surprisingly child-friendly city. Earlier in this chapter I talked at length about the City of Arts and Sciences (see p 22–p 25), which is a must for children, but Valencia has plenty more to offer. If you are here in summer, and actually even in winter, there are play areas all over the beaches and in the public parks. Many museums dedicate Saturdays or Sundays to children's workshops, and of course, the city's marvelous sandy beaches will keep young ones amused for hours. START: Bus 95 to Avenida Peris y Valero.

1 ★★★ kids **Parque Gulliver.** A huge Gulliver (from Swift's *Gulliver's Travels*) makes up the 'body' of this playground. He lies sprawled on his back, tied to the ground, with his body and clothing as slides and climbing sections that allow the children to become Lilliputians. I'm often tempted to have a go myself! This fantastic place is in the Río Túria Park. Kids (and adults) will also love the life-size chessboards and the skateboard park nearby. ⏱ *1 hr+. Entrance by Puente Angel Custodio. Avda Peris y Valero. Admission free. Bus: 95.*

2 ★★★ kids **Centro Cultural la Beneficencia.** This houses one of my very favorite museums, the Museum of Ethnology. Most weekends they have a range of workshops and entertainment for children such as music, clowns, and model-making. Even if there are no activities during your visit, the exhibitions are brilliant for kids: models of houses, costume, machinery, and games through the ages. ⏱ *45 min. C/ Corona, 36. 46003.* ☎ *96-388-3614. See p 17, bullet* **3***, p 40, bullet* **11***.*

3 **Cafeteria Beneficencia.** Sit in the Beneficencia's central courtyard, all blue-and-white tiles and giant rubber plants, and indulge in a coffee or a drink and tapas while the kids are looked after. *C/ Corona, 36. No phone. $.*

4 ★★★ kids **Jardines del Real/ Jardines de Viveros.** Another favorite, these gardens are sure to keep the kids amused, there is a section especially for children called Tráfico, a clever road system in miniature that teaches children road sense in a fun way (your kids will need to take their own bikes). The Museo de Ciencias Naturales (Natural Science) is also here—very child-friendly with lots of fun, hands-on activities. ⏱ *2 hr. Entrance by Puente Real. Open 8am–sunset. Bus: 1, 5b, 6, 8, 11, 16, 26, 28, 29, 36, 79, 95.*

5 ★★★ kids **Bioparc.** This new zoo is a fine place to take children to teach them about the environment and animals in the wild. It uses 'zoo-immersion' technology, which basically means that you are

Lemurs in the Bioparc.

unaware that the animals are caged; it's a unique and very clever concept. 🕐 *3 hr. Avda. Pío Baroja, 3. www.bioparcvalencia.es. Admission 20€ adults, 15€ children. Daily 10am–8pm. Metro: Nou D'Octubre. Bus: 7, 17, 29, 61, 81, 95. See bullet ❶, p 13.*

6 Bioparc Cafeteria/Restaurant. This is a brilliant copy of a thatched African bush house where you eat on a terrace that overlooks a 'waterhole' where antelope, giraffes, and other animals come to drink. In the distance the lions, who can look but cannot touch, prowl. *Avda. Pío Baroja, 3. No phone. $$.*

7 ★★ kids Parque Cabecera. This is the park in which the Bioparc resides. A massive 4,145 trees, 31,000 shrubs, and 73,000 wildflowers have been planted to make this new park. The lake at its center has huge swan-shaped pedalos and canoes for hire. It's a lovely spot to watch the wildfowl, and look out for the huge turtles in the water. Take one of the park's three suggested walks—you'll find the routes on

Swan pedalos at Parque Cabecera.

posts around the park. Be sure to take the spiral path up past the amphitheater for the views from 'La Montaña'. 🕐 *2 hr. C/ Pío Baroja. No phone. Open 24hrs. Bus: 95. See page 77, bullet ❶.*

8 Wiki Cafeteria/Restaurant. Built into the wall on the quayside of the lake, this bar does good tapas, and meals. Open all day from breakfast to dinner and in the summer months until the very early hours. *C/Pío Baroja.* ☎ *65-685-6899. $$.*

9 ★★★ kids Theme parks. If you want to experience white-knuckle thrills, you will need to get to one of the 'Benis': Benicassim in the north or Benidorm in the south. Benicassim, an hour's drive from Valencia (a fast train, too) has **Aquarama** with water chutes, slides, surf beaches, and a space shot, among a host of other attractions. Benidorm, just over an hour's drive from the city, has **Terra Mitica**, a thrill-a-minute journey through the ancient worlds of Rome, Greece, Iberia, and Egypt. The 360-degree corkscrews and

Attraction at Terra Mitica.

loops, 60miles/100km-an-hour upside-down and nosedive falls, are just some of the attractions on offer. Up to 50 daily shows, concerts, and blockbuster musicals are staged throughout the park. There are no trains to Benidorm, but there are good daily luxury coach services, taking about two hours each way. (See day trips p 137) ⏱ *A day out. Aquarama* ☎ 96-430-3321. *www. aquarama.net. Daily 11am–7pm Jun 14–Sept 7. Admission: 18.00€ adults; 12.50€ children, senior citizens, & disabled. 1 hr train from Estación Norte. Terra Mitica* ☎ 90-202-0220. *www.terramiticapark.com. Daily 10am–1am high season. Admission: 34€ adults; 25.50€ children, senior citizens; 22€ disabled.*

⑩ ★★ kids **Polideportivos.** If you fancy a change from the beach, the majority of villages around Valencia have *polideportivos* (sports centers), which are open to the general public. They generally feature outdoor swimming pools, sunbathing areas, tennis and fronton courts, and, sometimes, gyms, and almost all have a bar/restaurant attached. A day in one will cost you a couple of euros a head and a set lunch as little as 8€ including drinks. My wife and I try new ones out each summer. A recent find is the one at **Cheste**, half an hour's train-ride away, which has no less than three pools. ⏱ *4 hr. or more. Cheste: Ctra Cheste-Chiva,s/n.* ☎ *67-155-1342. 10am–6pm Jun 15–Sept 15. Half an hour's drive on Autovia A3 from Valencia or a train from Estación Norte.*

⑪ ★ **Restaurante Me Quedo en la Parra.** This bar/restaurant is typical of establishments attached to *polideportivos* (sports centers). Spotlessly clean and very well run, the staff is cheerful and friendly. The food is all home cooked, very inexpensive and consistently good. The terrace looks over the three pools and gardens. *Ctra Cheste-Chia,s/n.* ☎ *67-155-1342. $$.*

Valencia for the Culture Vulture

1 Iglesia de San Juan del Hospital
2 Iglesia de San Esteve
3 Iglesia de Santa Catalina
4 Iglesia del Carmen
5 Café Museu
6 Museu L'Iber
7 IVAM - Institut Valencià d'Art Modern
8 La Sucursal
9 MUVIM - Museu Valencià de la Il·lustració i la Modernitat
10 Museo de Bellas Artes de Valencia, San Pio V
11 Centro Cultural la Beneficencia

(i) Information
✉ Post Office
Ⓜ Metro Station

For a city that remained forgotten for so long, it is amazing just how much there is to see for the art lover. It is not just the museums and galleries (no less than 28 public and numerous private galleries), but churches and palaces from almost every epoch will thrill even the most jaded eye. This tour starts with my favorite churches, which are generally open to the public all day, to view or worship in. If you like to light a candle when you enter a church, you may be disappointed, electric candles have taken over—a coin in the slot buys a few moments of flickering light. Next, we'll go to what I consider to be the best museums and galleries. But wherever you are, don't forget to look up—there are visual treasures to be seen all over the city and if you see an open church or a museum I haven't mentioned, take a look inside. START: **31, 36, 70, 71 Bus to C/La Paz.**

❶ ★★★ Iglesia de San Juan del Hospital. Founded by King Jaime 1 in 1238 and given to the Knights of the Order of Malta, this is said to be the oldest church in the city and is my favorite. You enter through an arch, where the mark of the order is still preserved on the wall, to a peaceful courtyard. The main door to the very simple nave is at the rear. Opus Dei is restoring it, after years of neglect. There is a weekly English Saturday service. ⏱ *1 hr. C/ Trinquete de Caballeros 5.* ☎ *96-392-2965. 9.30am–1.30pm & 5–9.30pm Mon–Sat, 11am–1.30pm & 5–9.30pm Sun. Bus: 31, 36, 70, 71.*

❷ ★ Iglesia de San Esteve. Just off the Plaza de la Virgen, this

Iglesia de Santa Catalina.

rather dour-looking church is a revelation inside. Although it is one of the oldest in the city, the inside was remodeled in the 18th century and the amount of gold leaf from floor to ceiling on the intricate Baroque relief plasterwork is astounding. The church is very popular for christenings—San Vicente the Martyr is said to have used the baptismal font, and legend has it that it gives protection to those who are baptized in it. ⏱ *15 min. Plaza San Esteve.* ☎ *96-391-8276. Open daily, times vary. Bus: 5.*

❸ ★★ kids Iglesia de Santa Catalina. Another fine example of Gothic architecture, said to have been the sixth church consecrated

Medieval jousting at Museu L'Iber.

by King Jaime 1 in the early 13th century. The church has had a checkered history: it was devastated by fire in the 16th century and then again during the Civil War. In 1950 work began on a complete restoration of the building when the architect Luis Gay Ramos stripped it of all its baroque embellishments. Its three naves are now pure Gothic. You can see salvaged pieces from its restoration cemented into an outside wall. Santa Catalina's bell tower is very close to the cathedral's tower, El Miguelete (see p 28, bullet ④), and so is lovingly known as Miguelete's wife. 🕐 *30 min. Plaza Santa Catalina.* ☎ *96-391-7713. Open daily.*

④ ★ kids **Iglesia del Carmen.** The façade of this imposing and impressive 17th-century landmark baroque church is crumbling a little, but is in the process of being restored. Unfortunately, inside there is not much of interest to see. However, this is a delightful plaza and, while you are here, you will notice a cacophony of screeching bird sound. If you look for the source of this noise, you will probably see more than a few green parakeets—a

colony roost in the belfry. 🕐 *15 min. Plaza de Carmen. Open daily. See p 52, bullet* ⑯.

⑤ **Café Museu.** This friendly little bar is frequented mainly by a hippy, local crowd, reflected in the price of the drink and tapas. It has a shady, breezy terrace on a virtually pedestrian-only street. *C/ Museu 7.* ☎ *96-393-3108. $–$$.*

⑥ ★★★ kids **Museu L'Iber.** This fantastic private collection of lead soldiers—more than one million of them—is housed in a beautiful, 15th-century neoclassical palace in Barrio del Carmen. There are dioramas of famous battle scenes, the Kings' Guards through history, including Franco's guards, and scenes from ancient history too— some little racy. Only a minute portion of the collection is currently on display, 1,000 sq m/11,000sq ft at present. By the time it is completed there will be a staggering 130,000sq ft/12,000sq m in total. 🕐 *1–2 hr. L'Iber, Calle Caballeros 20 and 22.* ☎ *963-91-0811. www.museo liber.org. Admission 4€. Wed–Fri*

11am–2pm & 4pm–8pm, weekends 11am–2pm & 3–8pm. Bus: 5b (see p 49, bullet ⑥).

⑦ ★★★ kids IVAM—Institut Valencià d'Art Modern.

Regarded as one of the best contemporary art spaces in the world, this museum is home to the work of Valencian sculptor Julio González among others and has a rich program of exhibitions, performances, concerts, workshops, and conferences. A huge and ambitious project is under way to almost double the size of IVAM with a clever box made of perforated steel that will cover the existing building. Check before you visit, there may be a concert in the entrance hall or on the steps outside. ⏱ *2 hr. C/ Guillém de Castro 118.* ☎ *96-386-3000. www.ivam.es. Admission 2€, students 1€, disabled free. Free Sun. Tues–Sun 10am–8pm. Bus: 5, 6, 62, tourist bus.*

⑧ La Sucursal.

Just as you'd expect in a restaurant housed in a modern art museum, the dining room is all white light and minimalism. The food is Mediterranean and specialist dishes here are *melosos*—quite delicious and delicate wet rice dishes, the best of which is the lobster, *Arroz Caldoso de Bogavante*. Good regional wine list too. *C/ Guillém de Castro 118.* ☎ *96-374-6665. $$$$$.*

⑨ ★★★ kids MUVIM—Museu Valencià de la Il·lustració i la Modernitat.

Literally translated, the name MUVIM is 'Valencia Museum of Enlightenment and Modernity', and is a permanent exhibition in the form of a multimedia show, (in four languages) whose subject is the European Age of Enlightenment. A brilliantly conceived and presented multimedia

collage of sound and vision takes you on a journey through history. There are also regular, innovative shows ranging from graphics to illustration, photography, and architecture. Advance booking is essential. ⏱ *1 hr+. C/ Guillém de Castro 8.* ☎ *96-388-3730. www.muvim.es. Admission free. Tues–Sat 10am–2pm & 4–8pm, Sun 10am–2pm. Bus: 5, 60.*

⑩ ★★★ kids Museo de Bellas Artes de Valencia, San Pío V.

This wonderful museum never disappoints and constantly surprises by staging original and fascinating temporary exhibitions of paintings and sculpture. The collection in this huge museum comprises works from as early as the 13th century to the early 20th century and is Spain's second most important art collection. Valencia's artists, unsurprisingly, are well represented, with works from painters including Juan de Joanes, Pinazo, Benlliure (see bullet ⑤, p 18) and the marvelous Joaquín Sorolla. But there are also works from such artists as Sarto, Van Dyck, Murillo, Velázquez, and Goya too. ⏱ *1 hr+. C/ San Pío V, 9.* ☎ *96-387-0300. www.cult.gva.es/mbav/es.htm. Admission free.*

IVAM—Institut Valencià d'Art Modern.

Museo de Bellas Artes de Valencia.

Tues–Sun 10am–8pm. Bus: 1, 5b, 6, 8, 11, 16, 26, 28, 29, 36, 79, 95, tourist bus.

⑪ ★★★ kids Centro Cultural la Beneficencia. Home to the splendid Museum of Ethnology and Museum of Prehistory; this cultural center was built in 1841 on the grounds of an old convent as an orphanage. In the middle of the cool courtyard is a beautiful neo-Byzantine church built in 1883 by Joaquin Maria Belda. I am afraid one prehistoric artifact is much like any other to me, so I have to admit that I have never spent much time in the Prehistory Museum, but it is a well-regarded museum showing the prehistory of Valencia from *Homo sapiens* to Roman times. The ethnology museum is much more to my liking. The permanent exhibition 'The Lived Town' is fascinating, and shows Valencia and its surroundings through recent history (mid-19th to mid-20th century). Performances here include world music, world cooking, and lost Valencian arts. ⏱ *45 min. C/ Corona, 36, 46003. www.museuvalenciaetnologia.es. ☎ 96-388-3614. Open daily 10am–8pm. Bus: 5, 60, 62. See p 17, bullet ❸, p 33, bullet ❷.* ●

Ensanche & Calle Colón

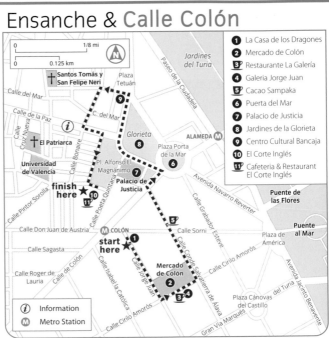

Map legend:
1. La Casa de los Dragones
2. Mercado de Colón
3. Restaurante La Galería
4. Galeria Jorge Juan
5. Cacao Sampaka
6. Puerta del Mar
7. Palacio de Justicia
8. Jardines de la Glorieta
9. Centro Cultural Bancaja
10. El Corte Inglés
11. Cafeteria & Restaurant El Corte Inglés

(i) Information
(M) Metro Station

Calle Colón is Valencia's main shopping street, crammed with department stores, fashion houses, chain stores, bars, and cafés. The streets that lead off it are full of smart shops and the occasional bar or restaurant. This area, known as Ensanche, is very fashionable nowadays and always has been. There are some very attractive residential buildings here, many of which are fine examples of Modernista architecture and design. The most interesting and unusual of these is the first on our walk. START: **Metro: Colón.**

① ★★ La Casa de los Dragones. As you come out of the metro station, turn right and walk to the pavement, stand with your back to the department store and look across the road, slightly to the left. Now look at the buildings carefully and you'll notice a very ornate pale yellow building. Yes, those are dragons holding up the balconies. The building is a riot of neo-Gothic elements including floral motifs, highly decorated columns raised on corbels, and a winged train, the latter representing progress. Much has been read into the star motif, but it is actually the logo of the-then Northern Railway Company. As you get closer you will see that the attention to detail is remarkable. The highly individual decoration of the façades is the very singular style of its designer, José Manuel Cortina Pérez (1868–1950), who built it in 1901 in what has been christened 'the

Medieval style'. Cortina is also responsible for two other exotic buildings close by (one round the corner in Calle Sorní 14, and the other in Calle Caballeros 8), but this is his masterpiece. ⏱ *10 min. C/ Jorge Juan. Metro: Colón.*

❷ ★★ **Mercado de Colón.** Walk down Calle Jorge Juan and you'll see ahead the Mercado de Colón, opened in 1916. It fell into neglect for decades, only to be reopened a few years ago. The restored mosaic images of farmland and its people are vibrant, the colors luscious and the detail meticulous. Sit and watch the world go by in one of the many cafés, bars, and *horchaterias*. At one end, there are two glass-canopied flower shops, selling everything from Bonsai olive trees to decorative palms, and huge electric flowerpots that light up at night. Downstairs, the central part is devoted to books and cds/dvds. You can also eat in the excellent Bamboo (see p. 94), hidden behind the glass waterfall. At the opposite end downstairs are some specialist food stalls—I occasionally treat myself to gourmet takeaway dishes from El Huevo de Colón, which is also a great place for foodie gifts (see p. 60). Free concerts and performances are put on regularly and I have, at one time or another, come across a tango teadance, brass bands (regularly), clowns and children's entertainers, and a grand piano recital. But at Christmas, the mercado is *the* place to get into the spirit of the season, when it is decorated and lit from head to toe. ⏱ *30 min. C/ Jorge Juan. No phone. www.mercadocolon.com. Daily 8.30am–1.30pm and some stores later. AE, MC, V. Bus: 12, 13. Metro: Colón.*

❸ ★★ **Restaurante La Galería.** This arrocería or rice restaurant has a plush dining room upstairs, but it

La Casa de los Dragones.

also has a coffee shop in the center of the main floor. Justly renowned for their paellas and rice dishes, at lunchtime during the week they offer a different, specially priced rice of the day. My personal favorite is their *Arroz de Verduras,* using every conceivable vegetable fresh from the fields around the city. *Mercado de Colón, C/ Conde de Salvatierra, 19.* ☎ *96-353-4062. $$$.*

❹ **Galeria Jorge Juan.** Across the street from the mercado is Galeria Jorge Juan, a small, chic shopping center selling designer clothes and jewelry and now dominated by Habitat. All around this area are side streets worth exploring for good shopping. Bear in mind, though, that the smaller shops in this area close between 2pm and 5pm, because it is siesta time. While you're here, look up and around you at the ornate buildings with wonderful plaster and ironwork, many of which remind me of decorated wedding cakes. ⏱ *20 min. C/ Jorge Juan 21.* ☎ *96-352-4966. www.lagaleria jorgejuan.com. Mon–Sat 10am–9pm.*

5 ★★ **Cacao Sampaka.** For our next stop on this short walk, leave Galeria Jorge Juan and walk to the flower shop end of the Mercado de Colón, turn left into Calle Code de Salvatierra. This is 'haute chocolat'! Chocolate for the gastronome, Cacao Sampaka has an attractive and very reasonable priced cafeteria serving sublime chocolate. *C/ Conde de Salvatierra, 19.* ☎ 96-353-4062. $$.

6 ★★ **Puerta del Mar.** From Cacao Sampako, continue along Calle Conde de Salvatierra and then turn right into Calle Colón. Ahead of you, standing triumphantly on the center of a large roundabout, is Puerta del Mar (Gate of the Sea), a magnificent arch once part of the city walls. The walls were demolished in the late 19th century to allow the city to expand. Puerta del Mar prior to this was indeed the 'gate to the sea', over the river by the Puente del Mar (Bridge of the Sea). On the point of driving, this roundabout is very odd and, indeed, just a tad dangerous. When you approach it by car from the other side, you can choose to go left or right around it. If you're planning to drive here, or even cross this road on foot, bear that in mind! ⏲ *10 min.*

Puerta del Mar.

7 **Palacio de Justicia.** As you walk towards this gate, to your left is the old Palacio de Justicia (law courts), declared a National Historic and Artistic Monument in 1982. An extraordinary neoclassical building, with pink and white painted bricks and mortar, it was originally a customs house, until 1828 when it became a tobacco-processing factory. In 1914 it became the Palacio de Justicia—a functioning courthouse, so not open to the public. ⏲ *5 min.* ☎ 96-387-8100.

8 **Jardines de la Glorieta.** Beyond the Palacio de Justicia are the Jardines de la Glorieta. Take a walk through the gardens to see, close up, the amazing and giant *ficus* trees—with their enormous trunks and aerial roots they could have starred in the movie *Jurassic Park*. The gardens are not particularly large, but are filled with several species of trees from around the world, among them the cedar, giant oak and magnolia. Stunning statuary abounds, including cooling ornamental fountains, so this makes it a pleasant place to stop and escape from the heat. ⏲ *15 min.*

9 ★★★ **Centro Cultural Bancaja.** There is a sign in the shape of Picasso carrying a portfolio in the

The giant ficus trees in the Jardines de la Glorieta.

Jardines de Glorieta pointing in the direction of a large white building. This is the Centro Cultural Bancaja (Caja Bank Cultural Center), which, in addition to holding groundbreaking and sometimes record-breaking temporary exhibitions, surprisingly holds the largest collection of Picasso's drawings in Spain. The gallery recently held an exhibition of the works of Joaquín Sorolla, probably Valencia's most famous artist. The exhibition was so popular that in the latter weeks it remained open through the night to cope with the crowds that flocked to see it. ⏱ *1 hr. Plaza de Tetuán, 23.* ☎ *96-387-5864. www.obrasocial.bancaja.es. Daily 9am–9pm. Admission varies.*

🔟 **El Corte Inglés.** Walk to your left and you will cross a busy road over to a continuation of the park with the back of the El Corte Inglés Department store where we started from up ahead. Depending on the time of the year, the store, and those surrounding it, are a beacon of bright lights with huge graphics up their sides, particularly during the festive season and the city's annual festivals Fallas and Feria de Julio. ⏱ *1 hr or more. El Corte Inglés is in three locations on C/ Colón and there are more around the city.* ☎ *90-112-2122. www.elcorteingles.es. Mon–Sat 10am–10pm.*

11️⃣ ★ **Cafeteria & Restaurant El Corte Inglés.** I don't think a visit to any city in Spain is complete without at least a coffee in a branch of this monster of a department store chain. The cafeteria is always on the top floor, and all of Valencia's seven branches have good views across the city. It's always busy with ladies-who-lunch, tired-looking shoppers grabbing a quick bite, couples sitting close together, and family parties out for the day. The food is decent, the menu never varies, and always includes *El Corti* (a club sandwich with a fried egg poking through a round hole in the top slice of bread). The Á la Carte restaurant is an oasis of calm, but is quite a bit more expensive. El Corte Inglés is in three locations on C/ Colón and there are more around the city. ☎ *90-112-2122. $$$.*

Sign for the Caja Bank Cultural Center.

Barrio del Carmen

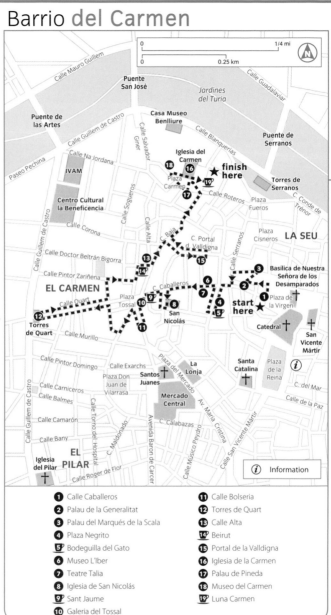

1. Calle Caballeros
2. Palau de la Generalitat
3. Palau del Marqués de la Scala
4. Plaza Negrito
5. Bodeguilla del Gato
6. Museo L'Iber
7. Teatre Talia
8. Iglesia de San Nicolás
9. Sant Jaume
10. Galeria del Tossal
11. Calle Bolseria
12. Torres de Quart
13. Calle Alta
14. Beirut
15. Portal de la Valldigna
16. Iglesia de la Carmen
17. Palau de Pineda
18. Museo del Carmen
19. Luna Carmen

The most historic and ancient part of the Centro Histórico is the Barrio del Carmen. It is also the most famous, and probably the most infamous, part of Valencia. Noted for its nightlife, everyone talks about it. Unfortunately, it has recently been a little emasculated by the strong *Vecinos* (Residents') Association who have ensured that almost everything closes by 2am. Not ideal when you consider that Valencians don't get going until 11pm or even midnight. Now, to stay out late, you have to go to other areas. Nonetheless it is still an interesting place to explore, both by day and by night. If you do the tour by day, start around 12.00 midday. By night to see the bars and restaurants in action around 10.00pm is a good time START: Bus 5 or 5b or walk to Plaza de la Virgen.

❶ Calle Caballeros. The Barrio del Carmen's main artery leads from La Plaza de la Virgen (see bullet ❻, p 29). This 'Street of the Knights', a bustling thoroughfare at the time of the conquest, when King Jaime I ejected the Moors from Valencia in 1208, is a narrow cobbled road lined with shops and bars. It is amazing to think many of the buildings are quite ancient, quite a few dating back to the 14th and 15th centuries. Narrow streets, some barely wide enough for a car, lead off taking you deep into a maze of more narrow streets

that make up this area. If you're walking here in the daytime, it can look like shutter-city—most of the bars only open at night and shops put down their shutters for siesta time between 2pm and 5pm. Be warned of the nasty, shin-height bollards used to stop cars trying to park—every time I walk down this street, I see at least one person bash into one. ⏱ *1–2 hr.*

❷ Palau de la Generalitat. The first thing you see on Calle Caballeros is this Gothic palace and its gardens

Hanging Out in the Barrio del Carmen

By day the Barrio del Carmen is a quiet maze of little streets, with a surprise around every corner in the form of a hole-in-the-wall bar, an ultra-chic, trendy clothes store, or a tiny shop that has been there for years (and without a lick of paint in all that time) selling bric-a-brac. By night, the area is heaving with all kinds of people out to have a good time. You'll encounter bars and small clubs that you probably didn't notice when you strolled around earlier in the day.

Like a lot of the Centro Histórico, the Barrio del Carmen is constantly changing—and it is particularly noticeable. Building work and signs proclaiming renovation appear on one building after another. When my wife and I first arrived here nine years ago, it was very sad to see many buildings literally on the point of falling down. Parts of the Carmen are still quite disheveled and in need of attention, but it is all coming together slowly—and it won't be very long before the whole barrio has been given a spit and polish.

St George on the wall of Palau de la Generalitat gardens.

filled with orange trees. Begun in 1421 and later completed by architect Pere Compte (1447–1506) who also designed La Lonja (see p 9, bullet ⑦), it has seen many new additions over the years. Its renaissance tower overlooks the Plaza de la Virgen and the last addition, another tower, was added in the 20th century. It is now the seat of the Valencian Government so not

open to the public. ⏱ *10 min. C/ Caballeros, 2.* ☎ *96-386-3461.*

❸ **Palau del Marqués de la Scala.** To the right of the Palau de la Generalitat is Plaza Manises with another fine Gothic palace, Palau del Marqués de la Scala. Originally built as a 16th-century stately home, it is currently the Valencia Provincial Council Headquarters. It has a wonderful courtyard garden, which you can see through the huge glass doors from the street on weekdays. ⏱ *5 min. Plaza Manises, 3.* ☎ *96-388-2500.*

❹ **Plaza Negrito.** Now take the second turning on the left, Calle Calatrava, and a short way down you'll come to Plaza Negrito, which is a terrace for the four bars that share it. Arguably, the most famous of these bars is Negritos with its eclectic mix of locals who drink alongside the growing number of visitors. You'll notice that there is also a palace on the square—if you're lucky enough, you might catch the owner arriving or leaving and get a view of the grand courtyard. Beware though, the

Adopt the Walk

My wife and I have adopted a particular method of walking round Barrio del Carmen. You might just find yourself doing it, too: walking along normally, then suddenly stopping and taking three reverse steps back to look at something that's caught your eye or indeed to change route altogether. I will explain. In this area, even the most ordinary and decrepit-looking building can suddenly reveal a marvelous and beautiful interior. If you're lucky, you might find one of the enormous front doors opened onto the street. Many of these buildings are centuries-old palaces and inside are myriad hidden treasures. I've walked down some of the streets a thousand times without seeing a door open and then one day it opens—and so I find myself quickly taking three reverse steps to catch a glimpse. If you do find a door open and have your camera, ask first before taking pictures. It is someone's home after all. So here's a tip: be prepared to 'adopt the walk'.

owner of this private palace does not like pictures being taken. ⏱ *10 min.*

⑤ Bodeguilla del Gato. This is just hidden from view as you walk into Plaza Negrito. A good, reasonably priced tapas menu and a well-chosen house red make this place a popular choice. If you go in the evening, be warned from around 9pm it gets busy so make sure you get there early. If it's full, put your name on the list, they'll tell you how long you'll need to wait and are usually fairly accurate. *C/ de Catalans, 10.* ☎ *96-391-8235. $$$.*

⑥ kids Museo L'Iber (The Museum of Lead Soldiers). Back up to Calle Caballeros now and turn left to continue our walk towards the central crossroads of the barrio, Plaza Tossal. Almost immediately, particularly if you look up, you will start seeing some fine façades. It has to be said that there is a huge amount of fly-posting and graffiti in the Carmen, some of it is actually commissioned and official,

some is most definitely not. On your right you will soon come to L'Iber, worth the price of the entrance if only to walk around this fine old palace. Though you will be pleasantly surprised at how interesting you'll find the exhibition of lead toy soldiers. (see p 38, bullet **⑥**).
⏱ *1 hr. Calle Caballeros 20/22.* ☎ *96-391-0811. www.museoliber. org. Wed–Fri 11am–2pm & 4–7pm. Sat/Sun 10am–3pm & 4–7pm. Admission 4€, under 4s free.*

⑦ Teatre Talia. On your right, almost directly opposite L'Iber you'll find Teatre Talia, one of three theaters that the government manages in the city. This one seats just under 400 and has a lively calendar of performances, including dance, mime, Spanish theater, and comedy. The restaurant on the first floor offers one of the cheapest *Menús del Día* in the city center—simple, basic fare and a bargain at under 6€ between 1.30 and 4pm. ⏱ *5 min— more if you stay for lunch! Calle Caballeros, 31.* ☎ *96-353-9260.*

Soldiers lined up at the Museu L'Iber.

Sant Jaume.

8 Iglesia de San Nicolás. A few meters on and, depending on the time of day, you may come across a stall selling religious artifacts and tracts on the same side of the street as the theater. Just next to this is a gate opening to a tiny alleyway, at the end of which, surprisingly, is a very large church, Iglesia de San Nicolás, which mixes both Gothic and Baroque architecture and was one of the first parish churches in the city following King Jaime's conquest in the 13th century. Adding to the impressiveness of the gloriously Baroque interior are the stunning frescos designed by Antonio Palomino (1653–1726) and painted for him by his contemporary, Dionís Vidal. Among the altar paintings is one by the Valencian Master Joan de Joanes (c. 1510–1579). The church stands on a delightful square of the same name, lined with particularly fine houses. Look out for the pale yellow house whose blocked-in windows have been painted with impressions of the scenes that might lie behind. They are very attractive and are worth the detour to see. ⏱ *20 min. C/ Caballeros 35.* ☎ *96-391-3317. 9am–1pm & 5-8pm.*

9 Sant Jaume. Back up to Caballeros and a little walk along on your left to a small tree-shaded plaza filled with tables (and usually people too) is one of our favorite bars in the Carmen, Sant Jaume. Converted from an old pharmacy with all the mirrors and shelving from the golden age of Spanish drugstores, this place is something of a Valencian landmark. Stop here to refuel and enjoy a refreshing drink (no food is served) as you watch the world go by. *C/ Caballeros, 51.* ☎ *96-391-2401. $.*

10 Galeria del Tossal. The Plaza del Tossal is at the end of Caballeros and is probably the most central point of the Carmen. Look for a raised square with a steel-and-glass structure with stairs going down that looks a little like a metro station. This is the Galeria del Tossal, a small museum where you can see a part of the Moorish city walls and recently excavated artifacts from the city's history. Worth a few minutes of your time; from time to time they stage interesting temporary exhibitions ranging from modern art to sculpture. ⏱ *20 min. Plaza del Tossal.* ☎ *96-398-1803. Tues–Sat 10am–2pm & 4.30–8.30pm. Sun/hols 10am–3pm. Admission 2€, Sat/Sun/hols free.*

11 Calle Bolseria. At the junction of Plaza del Tossal, head for Calle

Bolseria, a street lined with a real mix of shops, bars, eateries, and galleries. The shops range from high fashion to ones where time seems to have stood still: wool shops, an ancient old shop selling local honey (never, it seems, more than a few jars), and millinery shops selling everything from towels to overalls. The magnificent Modernista Mercado Central (Central Market) (see bullet **6**, p 9) and the 16th-century heritage building La Lonja (Silk Exchange) (see bullet **7**, p 9) are a two-minute walk further on. 🕐 *20 min.*

12 **kids** **Torres de Quart.** Head back to Plaza del Tossal and turn left into Calle Quart. It is worth a walk down its cobbles for more interesting architecture, good shopping, eating, and drinking, and to see the **Torres de Quart**, once part of the city walls and put to various uses down the centuries, including a prison and a storeroom. Climb to the top to look out over the barrio. See p 14, bullet **2** 🕐 *30 min. C/ Guillém de Castro 89. Admission free. Tues–Sun 10am–2pm & 4–8pm.*

13 **Calle Alta.** Head back to Plaza del Tossal and left up Calle Alta: a jacaranda tree-lined street that has restaurants and specialty shops down its length, such as classy take-away foods, arts and crafts shops,

Torres de Quart.

and a 'Condoneria' (a condom shop to you and me). There's even the Cañamaria restaurant, where each dish is said to be prepared with a 'toké' of marijuana. Down here on your left you will also see a doorway with the word Refugio over it, one of the shelters for use by the local population during the civil war. In a plaza just to the left off this street is the brand new Barrio del Carmen market, named after the plaza it stands in, **Mosen Sorell** (Mon to Sat 8am to 2pm). An attractive glasshouse full of inviting and interesting stalls selling fresh produce, fine wines, breads, and charcuterie, it has certainly lifted the look of this previously rather dingy square. 🕐 *20 min.*

Mercado Central.

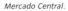

14 **Beirut.** This is an excellent local chain of Lebanese restaurants offering authentic Arabic food at reasonable prices. All the Lebanese favorites are to be found here: hummus, fatoush, taboulet, baba ganoush and they taste so good. They also offer a range of inexpensive wraps with tasty fillings that are perfect to take out or for a quick snack. Their taster menu for two is particularly good value, eight dishes with flat bread and a typical dessert for around *12€. Calle Alta, 10.* ☎ *96-391-8235. $$$.*

15 **Portal de la Valldigna.** You will need to check on our map to find this attraction, but it is well worth seeing. Walk from the market back to Calle Alta and cross through the little alley Calle Morella and left into Calle Baja, walk 30ft (9 meters) and turn right into Calle Portal de la Valldigna, you will soon see an archway with living accommodation above, it was built in the mid-15th century and was the gate to the Arab quarter when the city was still walled. A fresco is preserved under glass above the arch, and if you pass through and turn immediately right, you will see ahead of you a large rough lump of brick and stone several meters high, looking as if it could fall at any moment. It is, in fact, another relic of the original city walls. ⏱ *10 min.*

16 **Iglesia de la Carmen.** Make your way back the way you came and turn right toward the Río Túria. You will arrive at Plaza del Carmen, dominated by a large, slightly crumbling church, Iglesia de la Carmen, with its imposing façade. (See p 38, bullet **4**). ⏱ *10 min. Plaza del Carmen, 7.* ☎ *96-315-2024.*

17 **Palau de Pineda.** Turn left into the square, and to your left is Palau de Pineda, recently restored by Valencia University and now offering Spanish language and culture courses for foreigners, as well as a space for conferences and exhibitions. It has a charming courtyard café, open to the public. ⏱ *5 min. Plaza del Carmen, 4.* ☎ *96-386-9802.*

18 **Museo del Carmen.** Ahead of you, on the right, is the **Convento del Carmen,** now the Museo del Carmen, an art gallery and museum under the direction of the Museo de Bellas Artes (see p. 39, bullet **10**). This stunning building is a joy—a real and wonderful mix of architectural styles; parts of it date from the 13th century but the majority is 15th century. Within its walls are two beautiful, peaceful, and quite different cloisters, one Gothic and the other Renaissance. It is not just the fabric of this building that makes it so wonderful, it is also the excellent exhibitions and events that are staged on a regular basis here. It is regularly host to all kinds of avant-garde events and in recent years has been the 'stage' for stunning exhibitions, fashion shows, and some interesting experimental electronic art shows. ⏱ *1 hr. C/ Museu 2.* ☎ *96-315-2024. Bus: 5, 5b, 95.*

19 ★ **Luna Carmen.** As you sit down in this small, minimalist décor restaurant you will be handed a long sheet of paper and a pen. Tick off the dishes you want and the waiter will collect the paper from you and fulfill your order. Well-priced and prepared 'fusion' food. There are crepes and spring rolls with unusual fillings, fresh salads, and good fish. I always go for their excellent Thai green curry—currently there is no Thai restaurant in the city. In the summer months they have terrace tables, so you can literally dine under the *luna de Carmen* (Carmen moon). *Calle del Padre Huérfanos, 2.* ☎ *96-336-6213. $$$.* ●

Valencia Shopping

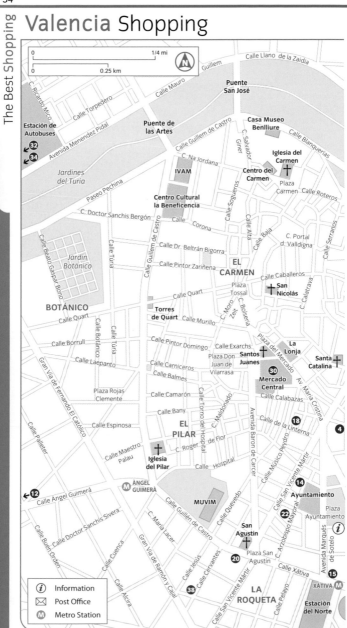

| 0 | 1/4 mi |
| 0 | 0.25 km |

Calle Llano de la Zaidia

Guillem

Calle Mauro

Puente
San José

Estación de
Autobuses
32
34
Avenida Menendez Pidal

C. Ricardo Mico

Calle Torpedero

Puente de
las Artes

Calle Guillem de Castro

C. Salvador

Giner

Casa Museo
Benlliure

Calle Blanquerias

Iglesia del
Carmen

Centro del
Carmen

Jardines
del Turia

Paseo Pechina

C. Na Jordana

IVAM

Calle Sogueros

Plaza
Carmen

Calle Roteros

Centro Cultural
la Beneficencia

C. Doctor Sanchis Bergón

Calle   Corona

Calle Alta

Calle Baja

C. Portal
d. Valldigna

Calle Serranos

Jardín
Botánico

Calle Turia

Calle Guillem de Castro

Calle Dr. Beltrán Bigorra

Calle Pintor Zariñena

EL
CARMEN

Calle Caballeros

San
Nicolás

C. Calatrava

BOTÁNICO

Calle Quart

Calle Quart

Torres
de Quart

Calle Murillo

Plaza
Tossal

C. Moro
Zeit

C. Bolseria

Calle Borrull

Calle Botánico

Calle Turia

Calle Laepanto

Calle Pintor Domingo

Calle Exarchs

Plaza Don
Juan de
Vilarrasa

Santos
Juanes

Plaza del Mercado

La
Lonja

Santa
Catalina

Av. Maria Cristina

Gran Via de Fernando El Católico

Beato Gaspar Bono

Calle Carniceros

Calle Balmes

30
Mercado
Central

Calle Calabazas

Plaza Rojas
Clemente

Calle Camarón

Calle Bany

EL
PILAR

Calle Torno del Hospital

C. Maldonado

Avenida Baron de Carcer

Calle de la Linterna

18

4

Calle Espinosa

C. Roger

de Flor

Calle Músico Peydro

Calle Maestro
Palau

Iglesia
del Pilar

Calle   Hospital

Calle San Vicente Mártir

14
Ayuntamiento

Calle Pallater

ÀNGEL
GUIMERÁ

Calle Ángel Guimerá

12

Calle Guillem de Castro

MUVIM

Calle Quevedo

22

C. Arabispo Mayoral

Plaza
Ayuntamiento

Calle Doctor Sanchis Sivera

C. Maria Lacer

Gran Via de Ramón y Cajal

San
Agustín

Avenida Marqués
de Sotelo

Calle Buen Orden

Calle Cuenca

Calle Alcira

Calle Jesús

Calle Cervantes

20

Plaza San
Agustín

38

Calle Xátiva

15

LA
ROQUETA

Calle San Vicente Mártir

Calle Pelayo

XÁTIVA

Estación
del Norte

(i) Information

⊠ Post Office

Ⓜ Metro Station

Abanicos Nela **1**
Adolfo Dominquez **2**
Alex Vidal **3**
Álvaro Moliner **4**
Antigüidades Marco Polo **5**
Aqua **6**
Bañon **7**
Bimba & Lola **8**
Cacao Sampaka **9**
Camper **10**
Carolina Herrera **11**
Centro Comercial Bonaire **12**
Centro Comercial El Saler **13**
Cool **14**
Cortefiel **15**
Druni **16**
El Corte Inglés **17**
El Globo **18**
El Huevo de Colón **19**
Fnac **20**
Goybal **21**
Herbolario J. Navarro **22**

Imaginarium **23**
J. Camps **24**
La Casa del Libro **25**
Lladró **26**
Loewe **27**
Louis Vuitton **28**
Mangland **29**
Mercado Central **30**
Mercado de Colón **31**
Mercado de Fuencarral **32**
Montesinos **33**
Nuevo Centro **34**
Papos **35**
Purificación Garcia **36**
Skateworld **37**
Spabrus **38**
Tous **39**
Ulanka **40**
Valencia Club de Futbol Shop **41**
Yacare **42**
Zara **43**
Zara Home **44**

Calle Sagunto
Calle Manyá

PONT DE FUSTA Ⓜ

Puente de Serranos
Real Monasterio de la Trinidad

Calle Conde de Trénor

Torres de Serranos

Puente Trinidad

Plaza Cisneros **㉑**

LA SEU

C. Salvador
C. Trinitarios

Basilica de Nuestra Señora de los Desamparados

Almudin

Plaza de la Virgen

Museo de La Ciudad

Catedral †

⑤

San Vicente Mártir

LA XEREA

Plaza de la Reina ⓘ

Calle del Mar

Santos Tomás y San Felipe Neri

Plaza Tetuán

Jardines del Turia

Paseo de la Ciudadela

Paseo de la Alameda

⑪ Calle de la Paz

Museo de Cerámica

㊱ **㉗**

El Patriarca † ⓘ

Glorieta

Puente de la Exposición

Ⓜ ALAMEDA

㉘

Universidad de Valencia

Plaza Alfonso El Magnánimo

Plaza Porta de la Mar

Avenida Navarro Reverter

㊲

Plaza Rodrigo Botet

C. Poeta Querol

㉖

Sorolla **㊶**

Puente de las Flores

ⓘ

Calle Barcas

C. Don Juan de Austria

Ⓜ COLÓN

⑰

Calle Poeta Quintana

⑨

㉝

Calle Grabador Esteve

Calle Sorni

Plaza de América

Calle Correos

Calle Sagasta

㊳ **㉟**

Calle de Colón

⑦

⑧

Calle Conde Salvatierra de Álava

Avenida Jacinto Benavente

✉

㊵

Calle Pascual y Genis

Lauria

EL PLA DEL REMEI

㉓

⑲ **㉙**

㉛

Calle Roger de Lauria

⑩

Calle Pizarro

Calle Hernán Cortés

Calle Almirante Cadarso

Calle Joaquín Costa

Mercado de Colón

Plaza Cánovas del Castillo

Calle Ribera

Paseo Ruzafa

㊹

②

③

Calle Cirilo Amorós

GRAN VIA

⑯

㊸ **㉕**

Calle Félix Pizcueta

Calle Martí

Gran Via Marqués del Turia

Calle Conde de Altea

Calle Císcar

Calle Conde de Altea

Calle Salamanca

Plaza de Toros

Calle Ruzafa

⑥ **⑬**

Shopping Best Bets

Best for Improbable Chocolate
★ Cacao Sampaka, C/ Conde de Salvatierra, 19 (p 60)

Best Designer Boutique
★★ Alex Vidal, C/ Hernán Cortes, 13 (p 59)

Best Bookshop
★ La Casa del Libro, Paseo Ruzafa 11 (p 57)

Best Fresh Produce
★★★ Mercado Central, Plaza Mercado (p 61)

Best Everything-Under-One-Roof
★ El Corte Inglés, C/ Colón (p 57)

Best Cosmetics & Fragrances
Druni, Paseo Ruzafa 11 (p 57)

Best Bargain Shoes
Ulanka, C/ Don Juan de Austria (p 67)

Best Fans for Men & Women
Abanicos Nela, C/ San Vicente Martir 2 (p 63)

Best Quality Shoes
★★ Yacare, C/ Jorge Juan 8 (p 67)

Best Souvenirs & Gifts
★ Goybal, C/ Muro de Santa Ana 4 (p 62)

Best Mall for Hipsters
★ Mercado de Fuencarral, Avda. Tirso de Molina, 16 (p 66)

Best Designer Babies-to-Teens
★★ Papos, C/ Pérez Bayer 9 (p 65)

Best Magpie Jewelry
Spabrus, C/ Troya 10 (p 63)

Most Luxury Accessories
★★★ Bimba & Lola, C/ Jorge Juan 17 (p 59)

Best Real Toys
★★ Imaginarium, C/ Jorge Juan 19 (p 64)

Best Hi Tech, Music & Entertainment
★ Fnac, C/ Guillém de Castro, 9-11 (p 57)

Best Inexpensive Designer Clothing
★★ Zara, Paseo Ruzafa 20 (p 59)

Best Gourmet Takeout & Designer Foodie Gifts
★★ El Huevo de Colón, Mercado de Colón (p 60)

Find everything under one roof at El Corte Inglés.

Valencia Shopping A to Z

Antiques
★★★Antigüidades Marco Polo CENTRO The stock here is fascinating, where huge religious artifacts vie with Modernista sculpture and paintings for your attention in the shop windows. Passing this shop always tests my willpower: I'm unable to walk by without wanting at least one beautiful object or work of art. *Plaza de Arzobispoa 11.* ☎ *96-352-7162. AE, MC, V. Bus: 5b. Map p 54.*

Books & CDs
★★ El Corte Inglés, Mercado de Colón CENTRO Downstairs in this wonderful Modernista/Art Nouveau building, you'll find a good selection of CDs, DVDs, and books (in Spanish only). Part of El Corte Inglés, it's good for a pleasant browse, especially if someone is playing the grand piano by the fountain. *Mercado de Colón, C/ Jorge Juan.* ☎ *96-350-9048. AE, DC, MC, V. Bus: 12, 13. Metro: Colón. Map p 54.*

★ Fnac CENTRO This fabulous shop, originating from France, has everything you could possibly need for entertainment: music, mp3 players, cameras, DVDs, and ticket sales for live concerts, as well as a selection of books in English, French, and German. They also have a coffee shop, and it is one of the very few shops open on Sunday in Valencia.

C/ Guillém de Castro, 9–11. ☎ *93-317-1336. www.fnac.es. MC, V. Bus: 7, 27, 28, 60. Metro: Angel Guimerá. Map p 54.*

La Casa del Libro CENTRO If you are a book lover like me, it is a little frustrating that there are not that many places to buy books in English in Valencia. However, La Casa del Libro has a surprisingly good selection. Well stocked and well laid out, it has a really nice 'booky' atmosphere. The staff are helpful and friendly, and there is a coffee shop on the first of its four floors. *Paseo Ruzafa 11.* ☎ *90-202-6411. www.casadellibro.com. MC, V. Bus: 5, 10, 13, 32, 81. Map p 54.*

Cosmetics
★★ Druni CENTRO At this Spanish chain, you'll find all the leading names in perfumes, cosmetics, and make-up: testers, advice, and makeovers, all in one attractive store. Look out for special offers on certain lines. This is the biggest of many branches in the city. *C/ Paseo Ruzafa 11.* ☎ *96-352-7162. AE, MC, V. Bus: 5, 32, 62, 81. Metro: Colón. Map p 54.*

Department Stores
El Corte Inglés CENTRO There are no less than seven branches of this department store chain in

Shopping for Antiques

I've listed my favorite antique shop only, but Valencia has many more worth seeking out. For the better ones, wander around the streets behind the cathedral, especially Calle Avellanas and the Plaza de Arzobispo or Calles Calatrava and Corretgeria in the Carmen.

Valencia alone. You'll find everything you need under one roof from a tube of toothpaste to a house! Most branches have excellent supermarkets, and very good cafeterias and restaurants, too. The supermarkets stock more unusual and foreign foods than most others, and interpreters are on hand if you need any help. The three most central stores are listed below. Dial any of their numbers for more information. *C/ Colón 1, young fashion.* ☎ *96-315-9549. Colón 27 household.* ☎ *96-351-3475. Pintor Sorolla, 26.* ☎ *96-315-9500. AE, DC, MC, V. www.elcorte ingles.es. Bus: 5, 10, 13, 32, 81. Metro: Colón. Map p 54.*

Fallas Shops

Álvaro Moliner CENTRO The industry that supports Las Fallas (see p 122), the fiesta that takes place in March each year, is enormous. There are towns devoted to weaving the fantastic brocades and silks for the Fallera's costumes. Some of the best shops to see and buy these beautiful fabrics and the accessories that are a vital part of Fallas are off Plaza de la Reina. This one has delightful examples of everything, from fabrics to dresses and hair accessories and shoes. *Pasaje Ripalda 18.* ☎ *96-351-4190.*

www.autonomas-ata.com/alvaro moliner/. AE, MC, V. Bus: 17, 19, 61. Metro: Xàtiva. Map p 54.

Fashion

★ Carolina Herrera CENTRO Venezuelan Carolina Herrera clothes are available in this maple-clad store on Calle La Paz at the beginning of the Golden Mile. Exclusive to Spain accessories are also on sale, branded with the CH logo, as well as bags, jewelry, and more. *C/ La Paz 5.* ☎ *96-315-3164. www.carolinaherrera.com. AE, DC, MC, V. Bus: 4, 6, 8, 9, 11, 70, 71. Map p 54.*

★ Cool CENTRO Aptly named stores right in the heart of the city; two shops offer designer collections for men and women from a host of exclusive brands including Colcci, Denny, Scotch and Soda, Nike, Puma, Dolce & Gabbana and more. *C/ San Vicente Mártir 35 and 57.* ☎ *96-353-6481. www.coolfashionable.es. Bus: 17, 19. Metro: Xàtiva.*

★ Cortefiel CENTRO Sophisticated clothes for the sophisticated lady and gentleman: smart and country casual. Check out the designer Pedro del Hierro for exclusive and outrageous designs. Shop here for unusual accessories, bags,

Fallera's costumes.

belts, and jewelry. *C/ Marqués De Sotelo 13.* ☎ *96-351-5619. www. cortefiel.es.AE, DC, MC, V. Bus: 5, 32, 62. Metro: Xàtiva. Map p 54.*

★ **Louis Vuitton** CENTRO This world-renowned label, one of the oldest fashion houses in the world, opened its beautiful store on a corner of the 'Golden Mile' just in time for the America's Cup, for which it was the official sponsor in 2007. *C/ Poeta Querol 5.* ☎ *96-351-2883. Bus: 26, 31.*

★★ **Zara** CENTRO Zara is part of an extraordinary Spanish empire and produces bang-on-trend clothing and accessories for men, women, and children. The stylish accessories and shoes are to die for. The best bit is that the beautifully designed clothes come at an affordable price. Although a huge chain, the turnover of stock is very fast, so it's rare that you'll bump into someone with the same outfit. A very clever company, there is a Zara at every corner. This one on Paseo Ruzafa is their newest and largest store in the city and has all their labels under one very big roof, including fabulous things for the house. *Paseo Ruzafa 20.* ☎ *96-351-7016. www.zara.com. AE, DC, MC, V. Bus: 5, 10, 13, 32, 62, 81. Metro: Colón. Map p 54.*

Fashion–Spanish Designers
★★ **Adolfo Dominguez** CENTRO A high quality Spanish brand with classic clothing for the fashion savvy of all ages. Dominguez is especially well known for his tailoring, for both men and women, which is sharp and has great detailing. Check out the ranges of unusual leather shoes and bags, too. *C/ Hernán Cortés, 12–14 & 31.* ☎ *96-351-9141 & 96-394-3812. AE, DC, MC, V. Bus: 2, 3, 4, 10, 80. Metro: Colón. Map p 54.*

★ **Alex Vidal** CENTRO Alex Vidal is a Valencian entrepreneur and fashion designer with several boutiques around the city. This is his largest store, spacious and chic, stocking not only his own ranges but international names, too: from Gucci to Versace, Cavalli to Alexander McQueen, and Lagerfeld to DSquared(3).Vidal's own lines are Alex Vidal, Alex Vidal Jr., Men, Women, and Couture. The young people who work in his stores are friendly and helpful, and are renowned for their rapport with the customers. *C/ Hernán Cortés, 132.* ☎ *96-342-7337. www.alexvidal. com.es/en. AE, DC, MC, V. Bus: 2, 3, 4, 10, 80. Metro: Colón.*

★ **Bimba & Lola** CENTRO Style and quality-wise, this is the closest you can get to designer without maxing out your credit card. Founded by Adolfo Dominguez's nieces, and aimed at 25- to 45-year-old women, the stores are styled like Parisian boutiques. Affordable chic without skimping on the glamour. *C/ Jorge Juan 17.* ☎ *96-394-4180. AE, DC, MC, V Bus: 2, 3, 5, 32, 41, 62, 80. Metro: Colón. Map p 54.*

★ **Loewe** CENTRO Beautifully cut clothes and luxury Spanish leather goods, high-brow fashion house Loewe is an absolute must. On the Golden Mile, the store is as gorgeous as the goods within. *C/ Poeta Querol, 7.* ☎ *96-353-3892. www. loewecentervalencia.com. AE, DC, MC, V. Bus: 4, 31, 70, 71. Map p 54.*

★★ **Montesinos** CENTRO Valencian born-and-bred Francis Montesinos's designs have a reputation for their innovativeness. The man himself can occasionally be spotted, looking a little like Salvador Dali, around the Barrio del Carmen. Montesinos was the pioneer of the skirt for men in Spain, and he regularly shocks with his new designs—this is not fashion for the faint hearted. His flagship store is in Canovas. *C/ Conde*

Shop like a local in the Mercado Central.

de Salvatierra, 25. ☎ 96-394-0612. *www.francismontesinos.com. AE, DC, MC, V. Bus: 1, 2, 3, 12, 13, 22, 41, 79. Metro: Colón. Map p 54.*

★ **Purificación Garcia** CENTRO Extremely elegant, unusual, and more than often delightfully quirky day and evening wear for ladies and men. Understated design at its very best. *C/ Colon 17.* ☎ 96-352-3606. *Bus: 5, 32, 62. Metro: Colón.*

Food

★ **Cacao Sampaka** CENTRO Chocolate your thing? Then Cacao Sampaka has to be high on your itinerary. The shop claims to use the best cocoas in the world to make the finest chocolate, using craftsmen trying out new ideas, techniques, and even flavors. Among the chocolatey things for sale are spreads, jams, sauces, and ice creams as well as chocolate powders, shavings, and tablets. The novelty here is the selection of flavorings on offer—some of the more unusual include flowers and herbs, Parmesan, black olive, and even anchovy! All are beautifully packaged and with absolutely no artificial preservatives. This gorgeously decadent shrine to chocolate also

has a little coffee bar—sorry, that should be a chocolate bar! *C/Conde de Salvatierra, 19.* ☎ 96-353-4062. *www.cacaosampaka.com. AE, MC, V. Bus: 2, 3, 5, 32, 41, 62, 80. Metro: Colón. Map p 54. See p 44.*

★ **El Huevo de Colón, Mercado de Colón** CENTRO A gourmet takeaway and gift food store selling beautifully prepared food. The prices range from around 25€ to 30€ for a main course and from as little as 2€ for a *tapa*. They also offer menus for special occasions and will cater any event. A first-rate selection of foodie gifts, too, from exotic oils and vinegars to foie gras and chocolate. *Mercado de Colón, C/ Jorge Juan.* ☎ 96-373-2949. *AE, MC, V. Bus: 12, 13. Metro: Colón. Map p 54.*

★ **Mangland, Mercado de Colón** CENTRO For the best *Iberica* hams, meats, sausage, and cheese from all over the Peninsula, this traditional delicatessen, founded in 1955, is hidden away, downstairs in Mercado de Colón. They will package any purchase for traveling. *Mercado de Colón, C/ Jorge Juan.* ☎ 96-352-8854. *MC, V. Bus: 12, 13. Metro: Colón. Map p 54.*

Something Special

Valencia is blessed with a selection of small independent shops that specialize in one particular area, such as fans, gloves, hats, or knives; there are even a couple that sell only string. Then there are the shops that sell all things religious—as you would expect, these are mainly around the cathedral. Worth checking out are the amazing shops that sell everything needed for Las Fallas (see p 122): materials, costumes, and all the accessories. It always amazes me how, even in the very touristy areas, these little shops thrive.

Health Store
Herbolario J. Navarro CENTRO
A wonderful emporium devoted to alternative, natural health products. Here you'll find vitamins, aloe vera products, specialty and herbal teas, foods, beauty products, and even a café. Until recently you could only find such products in small specialist shops and alternative fairs. Navarro offers a wide selection of products and trained staff are on hand to offer advice. There is also a calendar of courses and health advice days throughout the year. The café offers good teas and coffees and, of course, healthy meals,

too. They also do takeouts. *C/ Arzobispo Mayoral, 20 and C/ San Vicente 63.* ☎ *96-352-2851. www.terraverda. com. Bus: 17, 19. Metro: Xàtiva.*

Indoor Markets
Mercado Central CENTRO
Almost every barrio (area) in Valencia has its own covered market, but this is the mother of them all! Said to be the largest covered market in Europe, it is a haven for foodies. Almost 1,000 stalls sell high quality fresh meat, fish, fruit and vegetables, herbs and spices, and household goods—all at fair prices. It is a captivating place to shop or to browse.

Mercado de Colón.

Street & Flea Markets

Street markets in Valencia are numerous and take place on different days around the city, selling a wide array of products from clothes and shoes to elegant pottery and earthenware. Valencia's biggest street market opens on Tuesdays, near the main station, Estación del Norte. It starts on Calle Jerusalem and covers an enormous area in the streets around. Check at the tourist office for other areas.

The Spanish don't really go for second-hand goods in a big way, and instead tend to throw away old furniture. There is, however, a regular Sunday morning flea market in the car park of the old Mestalla Football Stadium in Avenida Aragón. It starts between 5am and 6am in the morning with bicycle sales. While some are legal, some are quite often stolen off the street. Later, from around 8am, the main trading gets going. A huge amount of junk is on offer but there's plenty of good stuff and sometimes genuine antiques. The official stalls each show their trader's license but there are always several illegal traders trying to pass off what are often stolen or fake goods. A word of warning: this is a busy market—keep an eye on your bag, wallet, and camera. It's probably best to leave everything but the minimum at your hotel.

Plaza Merced. ☎ *96-382-9101. AE, MC, V. Bus: 5b, 7, 27, 28, 60, 81. Metro: Xàtiva. Map p 54. See p 9, bullet* ❻.

Mercado de Colón

CENTRO   Once a food market serving the Colón area of the city, this market lay ruined for years and was restored in very recent years as a smart drinking and eating area. Restaurants and bars on the ground floor serve everything from *horchata* to cocktails and brunches to dinners. There is a smattering of good food stalls and a book and music store in the basement. *C/ Jorge Juan. No phone. www.mercado colon.com. Daily 8.30am–1.30pm and some stores later. AE, MC, V. Bus: 12, 13. Metro: Colón. Map p 54. See p 43, bullet* ❷.

Interiors & Homewares

★ **Bañon** CENTRO   From tiny little pieces of jewelry to large pieces of furniture, Bañon is a Valencian haven of goodies that has been offering fine goods since 1967. Everything for the home; from glass to ceramics and cutlery to lighting, from table linen to mirrors and frames, there are even things for the garden. Their jewelry and accessories make exquisite gifts for that special someone. Bañon have five stores in the center, some just specializing in accessories. *C/ Jorge Juan 5 & 13.* ☎ *96-394-0755. MC, V. Bus: 12, 13. Metro: Colón p 54.*

A Lladró design.

Decorative fan at Abanicos Nela.

★ **El Globo** CENTRO   A tiny frontage belies the incredible amount of stock piled high inside this basketware shop, which sells baskets to beaded curtains, seating to wooden toys and furniture. Founded in 1858, it is on a small pedestrian street and competes with several other shops selling similar stock—this one is my favorite. *C/ Música Peydró 16.* ☎ *96-352-6415. Bus: 7, 27, 28, 81.*

★ **Goybal** CENTRO   This is more of an emporium than a shop with a fabulous selection of furniture, furnishings, china, and decorative household wares. A family-run affair, it also offers a plethora of souvenirs; it has a table of the biggest selection of tiny gifts at pocket-money prices I have seen in the city. If all that wasn't enough, there an assortment of electrical goods; everything from hairdryers and food mixers to heaters and coffee makers. If you are here at Christmastime, they stock very pretty decorations, too. They also stock a good selection of religious artifacts. *C/ Muro de Santa Ana 4.* ☎ *96-391-9065. Bus: 5, 5b, 95.*

Lladró CENTRO   Known all over the world for its beautiful tall pale gray figurines in fine porcelain, Lladró, founded in the 1950s, is a Valencian company. The 'City of Porcelain' is in the town of Tavernes Blanques, just 20 minutes north of the city. The company has a beautiful store on Calle Poeta Querol where you can see all their ranges from the classical to their latest designs and themes, as well as their new selection of fragrances. Fascinating guided visits to The City of Porcelain (the museum and factory) are also available. Book by email or phone at least two weeks in advance, the tours are extremely popular. *Lladró Store C/ Poeta Querol 9.* ☎ *96-351-1625. The City of Porcelain, Tavernes Blanques. Mon–Thurs 9.30am–5pm, Fri 9.30am–1pm.* ☎ *90-021-1010 or 96-318-7008 or www.museo.lladro.com to book a tour. AE, MC, V. Metro: Jaume I. Map p 54.*

★ **Zara Home** CENTRO   Quality bed-linens in an assortment of colors, gorgeous blankets, Moroccan pouffes, crystal candlesticks, and picture frames—myriad elegant things to beautify your home. The trouble with this store is that every time my wife and I step in we just want to redecorate our home again. Zara Home baby/children section is full of more gorgeous things: wonderful hand-stitched patchwork quilts, delightful books, and interesting tableware. *C/ Jorge Juan 15.* ☎ *96-351-3252. AE, DC, MC, V. Bus: 5, 10, 13, 32, 81. Metro: Colón. See p 54.*

Spabrus.

Jewelry & Accessories

Abanicos Nela CENTRO   The fan is an essential accessory for not only women, but men too during the swelteringly hot summers and so there are, not surprisingly, shops that specialize in selling fans; this is one of our favorites. *C/ San Vicente Mártir 2.* ☎ *96-392-3023. AE, MC, V. Bus: 17, 19, 61. Metro: Xàtiva. Map p 54.*

J. Camps CENTRO   Almost directly opposite the fan shop is this little store selling mainly gloves. Gloves for all occasions and weathers. *C/ San Vicente Mártir 3.* ☎ *96-352-2526. AE, MC, V. Bus: 17, 19, 61. Metro: Xàtiva. Map p 54.*

★★ **Spabrus** CENTRO   This vivacious lady puts her life and soul into her two city-center stores. Small Aladdin's cave boutiques, they are gloriously decorated and carry a fabulous collection of eclectic jewelry. You will always find a piece you can't live without. Bought from designers all over the world, such as Pilgrim, Manouk, and Dal Blat, her clothing section is fun, pretty, original, and feminine. *C/Troya 10.* ☎ *96-353-0088. www.spabrus.com. AE, MC, V. Metro: Jesús. Map p 54.*

★ **Tous** CENTRO   Their signature logo is a very simple teddy bear silhouette, and it adorns jewelry, bags, shoes, phone holders, scarves, and

Shopping Hours & Sales

Most larger shops and stores in the city center open from 9.30am to 9pm. Some of the smaller, privately owned shops close from 2pm and reopen at 5pm. Very few shops open on Sundays, though there are exceptions when a Saint's day or Fiesta causes a shop to close on a weekday.

Sales (or *rebajas*) take place twice annually, starting in early January and again in early July. Discounts are usually very good, often starting at 50 percent off. For information on sales tax and related rebates for non E.U. residents, see p 163.

Shopping Areas

The majority of shops in this guide are on and around the streets of the historic center and Calle Colón; however, there are hundreds of beautiful shops all over the city. I have included a few of the top names in design, mainly the Spanish ones, but to find many more take a stroll along what is now called **'The Golden Mile'**, Calle Poeta Querol. The giant department store chain, El Corte Inglés (see p 57), with no less than seven stores within the city, has departments for the major international designers, too.

more. But the Tous teddy is not all there is on offer—their collections range from very understated gold and silver rings, necklaces, and earrings, to flower-, tulip-, heart- and, of course, teddy-emblazoned watches, bags, clothes, and perfumes. Dating back to the 1960s, this brand is a firm staple in every Spanish woman's jewelry box. If you visit their counter in El Corte Inglés, be sure to take a number from a dispenser and join the almost permanent queue. *C/ Colón, 70* ☎ *96-394-3990. www. tous.es. AE, DC, MC, V. Bus: 5, 10, 13, 32, 81. Metro: Colón. Map p 54.*

Kids Clothes & Toys

Imaginarium CENTRO   Step inside Imaginarium (either through the big door for big people or the little door for little ones) to discover a delightful shop filled with 'real' children's toys. Choose from dolls' houses, blowing bubbles, or papiermâché. A selection of wonderfully creative toys (there's no high-tech here) to entertain and educate any child. Aimed at children from 0 to 8 years and beyond—does one ever stop being a child, especially here? There are four Imaginariums in Valencia; well worth a visit. *C/ Jorge Juan 19.* ☎ *96-350-9048. AE, MC, V. Bus: 12, 13. Metro: Colón. Map p 54.*

★ **Papos** CENTRO   This is the place to go if you want your children to step out in serious style. Aside from their own brand of clothes, bags, and shoes, Papos stocks DKNY, D&G, Armani (and more) for children. The staff here are famous for making the shopping experience enjoyable for the whole family. *C/ Perez Bayer 9.* ☎ *96-352-2769. AE, MC, V. Bus: 5, 10, 13, 32, 81. Metro: Colón. Map p 54.*

Malls

Aqua CITY OF ARTS AND SCIENCES   This modern, new shopping mall is close to the City of Arts and Sciences, and is a good size and well designed. The big high street names are all here, as well as a few one-off designer shops to add to the mix. A variety of restaurants operate to cater to hungry shoppers and a grocery store is located in the basement. The ten-screen multiplex cinema completes the picture. Some people may feel nervous walking on the etched glass floors, particularly on the upper levels, but be assured they're very safe. *C/ Menorca 19.* ☎ *96-330-8429. Bus: 19, 20, 40. Map p 54.*

Centro Comercial Bonaire ALDAIA   Located close to the airport, it takes about 15 minutes by car or taxi to reach Bonaire. Unfortunately, by bus it takes nearly an hour. You will see villages en route that you might never see normally, but I don't think this compensates for the extra time added to the journey. Bonaire is billed as the biggest mall in Spain and is a monster of a place: shopping, outlets, food and drink, and entertainment, including bowling, a games area, and cinemas. The central shopping area is open-air and offers almost every well-known fashion chain. At the heart of this area is a two-storey food hall with a multitude of bars, fast-food joints, and restaurants selling a variety of cuisines. Upstairs is a multiplex cinema. Bonaire never seems to stop growing. Also on the complex are a Factory Outlet zone and electrical, computer, sports, and hardware superstores. A vast Alcampo hypermarket completes the picture—for the moment at least. *Autovia Ctra A-3, km 345.* ☎ *96-157-9224. www. bonaire.es. Map p 54.*

Centro Comercial El Saler CITY OF ARTS AND SCIENCES This mall also has the City of Arts and Sciences within sight but is located on the opposite side of the river to Aqua (see above). One of the older malls, yet one of the biggest, it is dominated by a huge Carrefour hypermarket. The huge assortment of shops and stores sell everything imaginable, while the extensive choice of fast-food bars and restaurants, a children's play park and a nine-screen multiplex cinema keep kids (or those tired with shopping) amused. *Autopista el Saler.* ☎ *96-395-7012. www.elsaler.com. Bus: 35, 95. Map p 54.*

★ **Mercado de Fuencarral** CAMPANAR When is a mall not a mall? This über-trendy shopping and entertainment center proclaims itself an anti-shopping center in its advertizing. It is stuffed with designer labels and chill-out zones with DJs spinning tunes and even boasts a restaurant called Laydown, where you do just that to eat—this is possibly Valencia's hippest zone. *Avenida Tirso de Molina, 16.* ☎ *96-317-3640. www. mdf.es. Bus: 29, 89, 95.*

Nuevo Centro BENIFERRI The 'New Center' was built in the 1970s and, to be honest, is crying out for a bit of a facelift. El Corte Inglés dominates this mall with a branch at either end and a quirky pyramid, selling DVDs, CDs, and concert

Everyday Essentials

The city center is very well served by the two main grocery store chains, Mercadona and Consum. Both have branches (quite often within spitting distance of each other) all over town and offer great value for money. Opening hours are 9am to 9.15pm Monday to Saturday. The 7–11 concept is just hitting Valencia. El Corte Inglés have tapped the niche and have opened SuperCor and OpenCor stores in residential areas, which sell food, fresh bread and patisserie, alcohol, magazines, and gifts. They open 364 days a year from 8am to 2pm, the maximum number of hours they are legally allowed. I had to be much more organized before this luxury arrived in Valencia.

One-of-a-kind products at Mercado Central.

tickets, in the center of the terraces. All the shops you need are here, including a good grocery store. Like Centro Comercial Bonaire (see left), this is an indoor/outdoor mall, and it is a perfect place to grab a drink or lunch from one of the many eateries or al fresco on their terraces. *Avenida Pio XII. ☎ 96-347-1642. www.nuevocentro.es. AE, DC, MC, V. Bus: 2, 22, 60, 61, 73, 79, 80, 95. Metro: Turia and Campanarú. Map p 54.*

One-of-a-Kind

Mercado Central CENTRO This is a fascinating shop, selling just string and raffia by the ball or the meter. This kind of store is becoming rarer around the city with the advent of office supplies chains and you wonder just how they survive. *C/ San Vicente Martir. ☎ 96-382-9101. AE, MC, V. Bus: 17, 19, 61. Metro: Xàtiva. Map p 54. See p 9.*

Shoes

★★ **Camper** CENTRO The cool Mallorcan designer footwear company Camper sell their original and comfortable shoes all over the world, but you will find them at least a third cheaper here. Soft, comfy, quirky, and fashionable—and simply a superb range. The shop is also quirky, just like the shoes. *C/ Colón, 13. ☎ 96-353-3955. AE, DC, MC, V. Bus: 5, 32, 62. Metro: Colón. Map p 54.*

★ **Ulanka** CENTRO If the other two shops are too extravagant for your taste and/or pocket, then Ulanka may just be what you want: high fashion shoes without breaking the bank. Ulanka can be found all over Valencia. *C/ Don Juan de Austria 9. ☎ 96-394-2391. AE, DC, MC, V. Bus: 5, 32, 62. Metro: Colón. Map 54.*

★ **Yacare** CENTRO One of the best selections of shoes in the city from the best of designers: Castañer, Hispanitas, Janet and Janet, Lodi, Paco Herrero. A must for shoe-lovers: you're sure to find something special and a little different. *C/ Jorge Juan, 8. ☎ 96-351-1802. AE, DC, MC, V. Bus: 5, 32, 62. Metro: Colón. Map p 54.*

Sporting Goods & Sportswear

Skateworld CENTRO Not just, as the name implies, skate gear, but also surf, ski, sail, roller or ice skating. All extreme sports are catered for

Valencia Club de Futbol Shop.

in both branches of Skateworld. All the best names for these specialist sports are stocked in these excellent stores. *C/ Comedias,14.* ☎ *96-353-1838 and Moratin, 7.* ☎ *96-394-4809. Bus: 31, 36, 70, 71.*

★**Valencia Club de Futbol Shop** CENTRO Valencia Football Club fans will be very happy in this city center store, specializing in all the gear for this highly successful team. Shirts, scarves, hats, football souvenirs of all kinds, and tickets for matches can also be purchased from here. If you miss the chance to shop here, they also have a smaller team shop at the airport. *C/ Pintor Sorolla 24.* ☎ *90-201-1919. Bus: 4, 5b, 6, 8, 9, 26, 28, 32. Metro: Colón.* ●

5

Rio Túria Park

BENICALAP Ⓜ   TRÀNSITS Ⓜ   Av. Dr. Peset Aleixandre   TORMOS

MARXALENES Ⓜ

Calle La Safor   Cortes Valencianas   Avinguda

SANT PAU   **EL CALVARI**   Jardin de Marxalenes   REUS Ⓜ

Avenida General Avilés   Avenida   Consellería de Cultura, Educacíon y Ciencia   Calle Padre Ferris   Avenida Burjasot   **MARXALENES**

Avenida Maestro Rodrigo   CAMPANAR-LA FE   Pío XII   Calle Joaquín Ballester   Puente San José

CAMPANAR   Avenida Campanar   Estación de Autobuses   Puente de Las Artes Ⓖ   Casa Museo Benlliure

C. Valle de la Ballestera   Avenida Menéndez Pidal   Pechina   IVAM   Iglesia del Carmen

TÚRIA Ⓜ   Av. Tirso de Molina   Puente de Ademuz   Jardines del Turia   Paseo   Centro Cultural la Beneficencia

Avenida Manuel de Falla   Puente de Campanar   Jardín Botánico   **EL CARMEN**   Calle Quart

Puente Nou d'Octubre   Paseo Pechina   **BOTÁNICO**   Calle Guillem de Castro   Torres de Quart   La Lonja

Calle Nou d'Octubre   Paseo Pechina   Calle Quart   Gran Vía de Fernando El Católico   Mercado Central

NOU MOLES   Calle Gabriel Miró   **EL PILAR**   Av. Baron de Cárcer

Avenida del Cid   AVENIDA DEL CID Ⓜ   Avenida Pérez Galdós   **EXTRAMURS**   Calle Ángel Guimerá   ÀNGEL GUIMERÁ Ⓜ   MUVIM   San Vicente Martír

Calle Linares   Avenida   Gran Vía de Ramón   **LA ROQUETA**

Calle Lorca   Calle del Cid   Calle San José de Calasanz   PLAZA ESPANYA Ⓜ   Estación del Norte

PATRAIX   Calle Tres Forques   Avenida Giorgeta   Calle Albacete   BAILÉN Ⓜ

Calle Salavert   Calle Cuenca   Calle San Vicente Martír

Calle Fontanares   **SAFRANAR**   JESÚS Ⓜ

Avenida Gaspar Aguilar   Calle Urgn   Calle Campos Crespo Ⓜ PATRAIX

FAVARA   Calle General Barroso   Calle San Vicente Martír   Calle de Oltá

---

❶ Puente L'Assut de l'Or
❷ Puente Monteolivete
❸ Museo Fallero
❹ Puente del Reino
❺ Puente del Ángel Custodio
❻ Palau de la Música
❼ Cafeteria Palau de la Música
❽ Puente de Aragón
❾ Puente del Mar
❿ Puente de las Flores
⓫ Puente de la Exposición
⓬ Puente del Real
⓭ Puente de la Trinidad
⓮ Puente de los Serranos
⓯ Puente de San José
⓰ Puente de las Artes
⓱ Puente de Ademuz, Puente de Campanar & Puente Nou d'Octubre

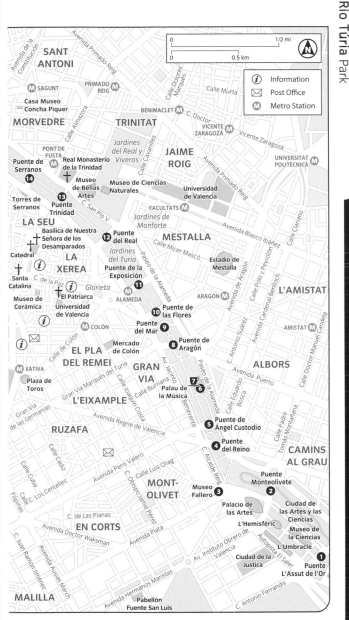

Let's take a walk up the Río Túria and look at the bridges. When the river was diverted to a new location and the old riverbed became a beautiful park, all the bridges were left in place to enable traffic to pass from one side of the city to the other. Some of them are ancient and are enchanting to view from above and below. We start from the lower end at La Ciudad de las Artes y las Ciencias up around the city to Parque Cabecera. START: **From the city center bus 19, 35, 40, or 95.**

1 ★★ **Puente L'Assut de l'Or.** Valencian architect Calatrava's latest creation is a tall suspension bridge, which separates the La Ciudad de las Artes y las Ciencias from El Àgora and the Oceanogràfic. It should be open from May 2009 and connects the newest districts of the city. ⏱ *10 min.*

2 ★ **Puente Monteolivete.** Walk up through the sculpture park or the Ciudad de las Artes y las Ciencias to this sweeping structure that separates L'Hemisfèric and Palau de les Arts. During Pope Benedict XVI's visit in June 2006 the bridge was closed to traffic while it held the podium and altar from which the Pope addressed the pilgrims that flooded the city. On the roundabout to the right is a very tall blue sculpture called *El Parotet*, by Valencian

artist and sculptor Miguel Navarro, who is responsible for the lovingly nicknamed *Pantera Rosa* (Pink Panther) sculpture on the other side of the city. People say it looks like the cartoon character from the title sequence of the Peter Sellers' film, but you need a vivid imagination in my opinion. ⏱ *10–20 min.*

3 ★★ **kids Museo Fallero.** Our first detour off the river, up to the left is the Fallas Festival Museum. Every year one of the *ninots*, or papier-mâché sculptures, is saved from flames by popular vote and is moved here to be displayed along with Fallas posters, photographs, and memorabilia. ⏱ *Up to 1 hr. 10am–2pm & 4.30–8.30pm Tues–Sat, 10am–3pm Sun & hols. Admission 2€, free entry on Sat, Sun & hols. Bus: 14, 15, 18, 35, 95.*

The Great Flood of 1957

Valencia has suffered flooding throughout the ages, a phenomenon known locally as *Gota Fría*, which, literally translated, means 'Cold Drop', referring to torrential rainfalls that happen in October and March. More than 40cm of rain in a 24-hour period is not uncommon. In the past, the Río Túria regularly broke its banks, but on October 14 1957 it did so for the last time, flooding and destroying vast parts of the city. The city fathers decided to divert the river away from the center of Valencia to a new, much wider flood channel around the north and west. With visionary foresight, they decided to keep the dry riverbed and all its bridges as a public park, which stretches more than 9km/5.7 miles from Parque Cabecera down to the Ciudad de las Artes y las Ciencias.

Home to Valencia's orchestra, the Palau de la Música.

4 ★★ Puente del Reino. This relatively new bridge, completed in 1999, is guarded at each end by wonderful 'fallen angels' with cat-like heads and soaring wings, as well as 126 eagle-head gargoyles down its length. Below the bridge is the children's playground Parque Gulliver (see p 33, bullet **1**) and a skateboard park. ⏱ *30 min.*

5 ★★ Puente del Ángel Custodio. A short walk on to the next bridge, a bit of a dull one this, although if you pass to the right-hand side of the river, the round-about at the end of the bridge has one of the curiously 'potato-head'-like sculptures by Castellón sculptor Juan Ripollés. This one represents books and reading. ⏱ *15 min.*

6 ★★★ kids Palau de la Música. Back down to the river and staying on this side, soon you will arrive at the home of the Orchestra of Valencia and the Municipal Brass Band, this is the main classical music center in the city. There are two auditoria and two smaller conference rooms. The public areas are all glass with orange trees planted in the pale marble floors. There is an excellent

bar overlooking the Palau gardens and fountains. ⏱ *20 min.*

7 ★ Cafeteria Palau de la Música. This excellent bar-café inside the Palau de la Música is a tempting place for refreshment and to watch the fountains. Upstairs there is also a bar in the orange-tree-filled glass house. *Paseo dela Alameda, s/n.* ☎ *96-337-2021. $$.*

8 ★ Puente de Aragón. Now we walk through pretty gardens and red-painted pools to this wide bridge that links Gran Vía Marques del Túria and Avenida de Aragón. Just before approaching the bridge on our walk, you'll see a large coat of arms of the city, vividly portrayed in plants, clearly showing *Lo Rat Penat* (the bat), the symbol of Valencia. The bridge affords a perfect view of it. ⏱ *15 min.*

9 ★★ Puente del Mar. Pass through more gardens to the pool under this ancient bridge. Built in the late 16th century, this beautiful stone 'Bridge of the Sea' was the main route from the city to the port and only became a pedestrian

The pond by the Puente del Mar.

bridge in 1933. Statues of the Virgin and San Pascual are sheltered by two triangular-roofed structures. The bridge is enormously popular with wedding parties and their photographers. ⏱ *10 min.*

⑩ ★★ kids Puente de las Flores. Just a few steps on to this pretty bridge, which links the city to L'Alameda and is lined all the way along on both sides with flowering plants, which are changed from season to season: poinsettias at Christmas time, cyclamen in winter and spring, and geraniums in the summer. The palm trees are planted below (not on), the bridge in the riverbed and come up through holes. ⏱ *5 min.*

⑪ ★★ kids Puente de la Exposición. If there is a celebration that requires fireworks (most of the time there is in Valencia), it is always between Puente de las Flores and here that they are let off for everyone to see—you can see the unplanted area from where they are let off on the way to the next bridge, also known as 'La Peineta' by locals because of its resemblance to an ornamental comb. Designed by Santiago Calatrava (architect of

CAC), the bridge runs above the Alameda metro station, which he also designed. It is worth a little detour down into the station to see what a master architect can do. I consider it more like a modern art gallery than a metro station. ⏱ *20 min.*

⑫ ★ Puente del Real. Pass by a football (soccer) pitch and the wooded area to another bridge rebuilt in the 16th century after the original wooden version was damaged by floods and became too dangerous to cross—although it took another 70 years for work to begin on the current one. Statues of two of the San Vicentes are here: Mártir and Ferrer. The bridge has recently been widened once again to cope with increased traffic, and the walls and statues have been restored. Come up to street level to enter the Royal Gardens (Viveros) and the wonderful Museo de Bellas Artes, the fine art museum (see p 39, bullet ⑩). ⏱ *20 min.*

⑬ ★ Puente de la Trinidad. Walk through some sculptures and lawns to the oldest of the Gothic bridges; it was built in the 14th century then reconstructed after the same flood that destroyed the Puente del Real. This bridge has also just recently been restored and widened. This area is full of football (soccer) pitches and at the weekend there are endless rounds of minor league football matches—all fascinating to watch. There is a footbridge along this section as well and some steep stairs up to the right, which lead to the old station Antigua Estación del Trenet, now a police station. Behind is the tram station where you can get trams to all over the network. ⏱ *15 min.*

⑭ ★ Puente de los Serranos. Now continue through more dirt football pitches and one smart new

Walk the Walk

If you do manage the whole walk you will have done better than me. I have only ever done it in sections, but every time I do, I see something new. All the way up from La Ciudad de las Artes y las Ciencias to Parque Cabecera, you will come across sculptures, cooling pools, and fountains.

Astroturf pitch to another of the city's oldest bridges. It was built by King Jaime's companions who came to conquer the city from Teruel in the 13th century. The bridge was their main entry to the city through the towers of the same name. To the left of this bridge is an ancient, stepped ramp, which is tough to walk up and down, but is worth the effort to take a look at the Torres de Serranos (see p 11, bullet **13**).
🕐 *20 min.*

15 ★ **Puente de San José.** The walk along the riverbed at this point is through a wooded area, wonderfully cool in the summer. The statue on this 17th-century bridge is of San José, patron saint of Fallas and

Father's Day, March 19 in Spain.
🕐 *15 min. See p 123.*

16 ★ **Puente de las Artes.** This bridge is next to Valencia's excellent Museum of Modern Art, IVAM (see p 18, bullet **4**). You can come up from the river and visit the gallery.
🕐 *15 min.*

17 **Puente de Ademuz, Puente de Campanar & Puente Nou d'Octubre.** The next three bridges are new road bridges and are really not worth mentioning. The walk between them is still interesting though. You will pass by baseball and rugby pitches, running tracks, and children's activity centers.
🕐 *30 min.*

The Peineta or Comb bridge by Santiago Calatrava.

Valencia's Parks & Gardens

ⓘ Information

✉ Post Office

Ⓜ Metro Station

1 Parque Cabecera
2 Café Wicky
3 Jardín Botánico
4 Jardín de las Hespérides
5 Jardines del Real
6 Jardín de Montforte
7 Paseo de la Alameda
8 Malvarrosa Beach
9 Chiringuitos

Valencia has a multitude of outdoor spaces, from the fabulous city beach at Malvarrosa to parks and gardens in an assortment of styles. Most of the parks run along either side of the huge Río Túria Park that we toured earlier. The parks are wonderful places to walk or laze in and almost all offer live entertainment throughout the year in the form of concerts, performances, open-air cinema or sporting events, and fiestas. Here, we begin at Parque Cabecera, Valencia's newest park and end the day on the beach. START: Metro to Nou D'Octubre.

1 ★★★ kids **Parque Cabecera.** Cabecera is Valencia's newest park and is actually at the top end of the 5.5 mile/9km river park, Río Túria. Built around a manmade lake, the 35-hectare park is divided into four main areas: a riverside forest; a lakeside Mediterranean garden; La Montaña, a mirador or viewpoint offering spectacular 360-degree views over the whole area; and finally Valencia's much acclaimed new zoo, the **Bioparc** (see bullet **1**, p 13). Vast swathes of green are home to an enormous array of trees, shrubs, and wildflowers, with paths and dry-stone walling running all the way through. You can hire a canoe or swan-shaped pedalo at the lake, which is stocked with fish and turtles. Radio-controlled model yachts sail by and I've seen several miniature America's Cup teams on the water at weekends. Suggested walks are signposted throughout the park, ranging from 10 to 30 minutes long. Children are extremely

Swan pedalos on the lake at Parque Cabecera.

well catered for, with the boating and also two good playgrounds. On

Bicycle Hire

Valencia is a relatively small and very flat city, which means that cycling around it is easy. There are a large number of cycle lanes in and around the city and various companies to rent bikes from; Orange Bikes on C/Editor Manuel Aguilar, (www.orangebikes.net ☎ 96-391-7551), have been around a long time, are reliable, and have really helpful staff.

History of Jardín Botánico

Jardín Botánico is the headquarters of the Escuela de Jardinería (School of Gardening) and is run by the University of Valencia, which describes it as a garden for science, culture, and nature. As one of the oldest gardens in the city, the University sowed its first plant here as early as 1567. For the first 200 years it was devoted to those with medicinal properties. In 1802 it was moved to its present location and was planted more generally. Although it began to fall into disrepair in the middle of the 20th century, it wasn't until the late 1980s that the task of restoring it was undertaken. The work was completed in 2002 and it now has among its various plants and trees one of the finest collections of palms in the country.

the way up the path that spirals around La Montaña, there is an amphitheater where, if you are lucky enough to be there at the right time, you might catch a concert or performance of some kind (see p 34, bullet ⑦). 🕐 *2–3 hr. Double that or more if you visit the Bioparc. Avda. Pío Baroja, 3. Open 24 hours. Free entry. Metro: Nou D'Octubre. Bus: 7, 17, 29, 61, 81, 95.*

2 ★ **Café Wicky.** On the lakeshore, this café is a very pleasant place to sit and watch the world go by over a drink, snack, or meal. In the summer it stays open to the small hours playing DJ-driven chill music and occasionally live music, too. *Parque Cabecera* ☎ *656-856-899. $$.*

3 ★★ **kids** **Jardín Botánico.** From the moment you enter the circular walkway, with a tree reaching through a hole to the heavens, you know this is going to be a special place. I particularly enjoy the gardens on a sunny Sunday morning, regardless of the time of year, when I have time to appreciate the seasonal changes of some 3,000 species of more than 7,000 plants, exotic trees

The umbracle in the Jardín Botánico.

Bathing statues in the Jardines del Real.

and palms, shrubs and bushes. The gardens are arranged into six zones—Medicinal, Citrus, Fruits, Farmland, Woods, and Industrial—and are laid out in neat square beds off a central pathway. There are tropical greenhouses and an impressive and ornate 19th-century cast-iron umbracle (tree house), which positively heaves with a jungle of greenery. I love the beds of huge spiky cactus plants and the Victorian greenhouse of rainforest plants, all steamy and exotic and dripping with condensation. There are regular art and sculpture exhibitions in the gallery building in the grounds, as well as workshops and conferences, courses, and free jazz concerts from time to time throughout the year.

🕐 *1–2 hr. C/ Quart–C/Beato Gaspar Bono.* ☎ *96-315-6800. www.jardin botanic.org. Daily 10am–9pm Mar– Sept; 10am–6pm Oct–Feb. 0.60€ adults, free up to age 7, senior citizens, students. Bus: 5, 5b, 95.*

4 ★★ **kids** Jardín de las Hespérides. Right next door to the Jardín Botánico is this relatively new garden, its outer walls lined with cypress trees. It is an attractive and very modern garden divided by linear water features. Sculptures of Hercules and Venus/Aphrodite combine with a dramatic use of marble,

Events in the Jardines del Real (Viveros)

At various times of the year, the park is host to a wide variety of exhibitions and events, from giant paellas and book fairs to dog training groups and Tai Chi—I recently saw a small group of people dressed as Native Americans, chanting and drumming! The annual film festival for young people, *Cinema Jove*, erects a screen in the park and shows several of its films in the open air. During the July Fair, *Feria de Julio*, an open-air stage and auditorium is set up and a month-long program of concerts featuring international artists, groups, and orchestras takes place under the stars.

Jardín de Montforte.

stone, concrete, and metal structures. More than 50 kinds of citrus tree are planted here, covering the eight groups in the genus from orange to pomelo. Some are extremely rare, having apparently been lost by the Jardín Botánico during the years of its decline. They are now being grown using almost-forgotten methods from the 15th century, as trees, in pots, and on trelliswork. ⏱ *1 hr. Between Jardín Botánico and Gran Vía Fernando el Católico. No phone. Daily Mar–Sept* *10am–8pm; Oct–Feb 10am–6pm. Admission free. Bus: 5, 5b, 95.*

⑤ Jardines del Real (Viveros). These were once the gardens of King Jaíme I's royal palace, which was demolished in 1810 during the War of Independence. In 1814 the rubble was piled up and formed into two small mounds called *Montañetta*, on which you can still sit and look over the park. *Viveros*, meaning "nursery", the name by which this large rambling park is commonly known, is

Out & About in the Sun

Valencia has more than 300 sunny days a year; the weather is so good here that the World Health Organization has officially recognized it to be a perfect climate for good health. It is no surprise then that there are so many outdoor leisure areas in the city; the Río Túria park covers over 5.5miles/9km of green space and there are parks and gardens all over. There are 17 officially designated natural parks and three protected natural marine reserves. There are forests and salt flats, palm groves and gorges, and wonderful beaches and coves along the entire coastline.

named so because in the late 19th and early 20th centuries it was used as a tree nursery. As you enter, to the left is a small lake with a waterfall at one end and a model of a heron at its center. Viveros is a quiet and calming place to saunter through, and has some very good cafés where you can stop for refreshments. The best part of the day for me here is siesta time, when it is often so quiet you feel you have the place to yourself. Among its attractions are a Natural Science Museum (see bullet ❹, p 33), a large rose garden, fountains and ponds, an aviary, several portals from palaces long gone, and some pleasing statuary. There is even a children's road system, where kids can experience riding their bikes in relative safety (see p 33, bullet ❹). ⏱ *2–3 hr. Calle Pio V. Open daily Mar–Sept 6.30am–8pm, Oct–Feb 8.30am–8.30pm. Bus: 1, 5, 5b, 26, 32, 79, 81.*

❻ **Jardin de Montforte.** This garden and palacette is a favorite of wedding couples, both for photos and civil weddings. Both the garden and palacette were originally built as a retreat by Juan Bautista in 1849. The gardens are open to the public, though, sadly, not the French Rococo-style palace. Among the varied styles is a geometric garden and rockery with paths running through it. The lions, which guard the small entry square to the gardens, were originally sculpted for the Madrid Parliament building. However, they were thought to be too small and were moved here instead. ⏱ *1 hr. C/ Montforte. Open daily Mar–Sept 10am–8pm, Oct–Feb 10am–6pm. Bus: 12, 29, 40, 80. Metro: Facultats then a short walk.*

❼ ★ kids **Paseo de la Alameda.** This stretch of the tree-lined avenue Paseo de la Alameda, from the Puente Real to the Puente de Flores, is a hub of activity throughout the year and accommodates (when the highway is closed) bike rides and races, marathons, parades, the Battle of the Flowers (see p 156), and of course, this being Valencia, fireworks (see box p 82). Although there is a six-lane highway at its center, this is a wide and attractive stretch. Charming cafés with terraces shelter under the trees with views across the river to the city. I particularly enjoy it here at sunset when, after a leisurely stroll, my wife and I sit and watch the sun go down over a *tinto* (glass of red wine).

Paseo de la Alameda

One street back from Paseo de la Alameda is Calle Galicia, which is worth a detour to see its buildings. The street is the site of the Regional Exhibition of 1909, and only three of the original buildings still stand, all of which have been beautifully renovated. These are the **7A Palacio de la Exposición,** an ornate Gothic masterpiece restored to full glory in 2002; **7B The Westin Valencia Hotel** (see p 136), which opened its doors in 2007; and the **7C *Tabacalera*** (tobacco factory) building, which will re-open as municipal offices. Back on the Alameda, the ornate stone bridge, **7D Puente del Mar** (see p 73, bullet 9) crosses the Río Túria park at this point. At weekends count the bridal parties having their photos taken, some days they are almost queuing. The next stretch runs behind the **7E Palau de la Música** (see p 73, bullet 6). Planted in 2002, this garden contains within its 5,500 sq m/ 59,000 sq ft all the flora of the Comunidad Valenciana. It is a living catalog of exotic and common Mediterranean plants, all pruned to form geometric shapes. ⏱ *45 min.*

⑧ ★★★ kids Malvarrosa Beach.

Until very recently Valencia was known as the city that turned its back on the sea. Then along came its big opportunity: to be host city to the America's Cup (see p 13). Valencia suddenly opened its eyes and saw an opportunity—it is now, very definitely, the city by the sea. The beach is within minutes of the city center by tram, metro, bus, or taxi. Valencia's huge stretch of beach is actually six separate beaches: Levante, Las Arenas, Malvarrosa, Cabanyal, Alboraya and Patacona, but locals consider it all as La Malvarrosa. It is one of many beaches that proudly bear a blue flag along the 392mile/632km coastline of the Comunidad Valenciana. The beach boasts clean, white sand and shallow waters. Lifeguards, showers, game nets, climbing frames, playground areas, and exercise apparatus are posted at regular intervals along its 2.5mile/4km length. It is very well equipped—along its palm-lined marble-paved promenade are seating areas, fountains, and drinking fountains. The beach is warm throughout the year, although natives tend not to swim before June or after the middle of September. *Tram: Dr Lluch or Las Arenas. Metro: Neptú. Bus: 1, 2, 20, 22, 23 (check timetables as some are seasonal).*

⑨ Chiringuitos.

Look out for these little beach bars, chiringuitos, selling drinks and small snacks that are all along the sands here. There are also bars and restaurants aplenty, the majority of which are at the marina end as well as further up the prom, where there are plenty of fast food places, too.

Malvarrosa beach and promenade.

L'Albufera: Beaches & Lagoon South of the City

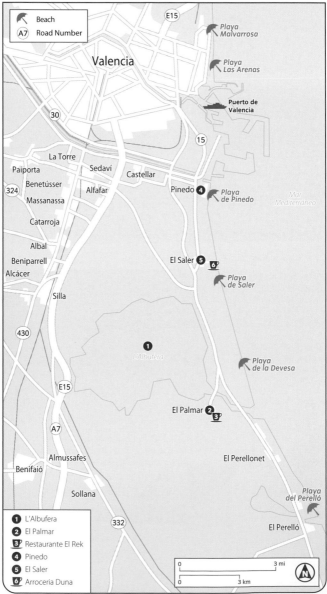

- Beach
- (A7) Road Number

Valencia

E15

Playa Malvarrosa

Playa Las Arenas

Puerto de Valencia

30

15

La Torre

Paiporta

Sedaví

Castellar

324

Benetússer

Alfafar

Massanassa

Pinedo ④

Playa de Pinedo

Mar Mediterráneo

Catarroja

Albal

Beniparrell

El Saler ⑤ ⑥

Alcácer

Playa de Saler

Silla

430

① L'Albufera

Playa de la Devesa

E15

A7

El Palmar ② ③

Almussafes

El Perellonet

Benifaió

Sollana

Playa del Perelló

332

El Perelló

- ① L'Albufera
- ② El Palmar
- ③ Restaurante El Rek
- ④ Pinedo
- ⑤ El Saler
- ⑥ Arroceria Duna

| 0 | 3 mi |
| 0 | 3 km |

When you stand on the shores of L'Albufera, the lagoon that irrigates the rice paddies that stretch for miles to the south, it is hard to believe that you are just a few minutes' drive from Valencia city center. This freshwater lake is at the center of what is now a Natural Park, a place to enjoy nature and protected for all time from further development. It is an outstanding place for a day out. There are lots of things to do: take a boat ride, have a picnic, or walk through the woods and on the beaches, eat in excellent restaurants, or just spot the wildlife. START: **Plaza de la Reina and get the Albufera tourist bus or the yellow Metrobus.**

Traditional barca waits for passengers on the Albufera.

❶ ★★★ kids L'Albufera. The best way to get to this beautiful lagoon is by car, or even by bike so you can spend the day exploring. L'Albufera is a huge 3,000 hectare lagoon, 6miles/11km to the south of the city and is surrounded by rice paddies. The lagoon was in danger of disappearing altogether until the area was given Natural Park status in 1986. If you look toward the narrow strip of land that separates it from the sea, you can see a cluster of high-rise blocks of flats. This development was planned to be much bigger, but once the Natural Park status was given, all further building stopped. Take a tour of the lake and its irrigation channels in a *barca (*a typical Albufera fisherman's

L'Albufera in Roman Times

L'Albufera was much larger back in Roman times, at 10 times the size it is now. To give you an idea of the scale of it then, Valencia Cathedral now stands roughly where the Temple to Diana stood on the banks of one of L'Albufera's islands. The lagoon would, of course, have reduced in size naturally over the centuries, but the reduction was accelerated in the 15th century when the Moors began to sow rice. Now the paddies occupy more than 14,000 hectares, all irrigated by the lagoon, though it is no longer enough to cope with local consumption. In fact, Valencia has to import rice from elsewhere to satisfy its citizens' lust for the product.

Sandy beach at El Palmar.

boat), it's a relaxing way to spend a few hours, doing something that hasn't changed for centuries. The rice paddies will look different throughout the year—sometimes swamped (September to February and April to June), sometimes dry and, in September, just before harvesting, a verdant green. It is very tranquil to watch the wildfowl and the water here. When you tire of just sitting, cross the road and take a walk through the pine-covered dunes to the sea, it is beautiful almost any day of the year. ⏱ *half day. 11km/6miles from Valencia, on the Albufera tourist bus from Plaza de la Reina or by car take the cv500.*

2 ★ **kids** **El Palmar.** At the southern edge of L'Albufera is the village of El Palmar, which is considered the spiritual home of Paella. The village boasts more *arrocerías* (rice restaurants) than almost anywhere in the Comunidad Valenciana. There are well over 20, which, for a village whose inhabitants number fewer than 900, is pretty good going. One large dining room after another, many seating 200 or more, all vie for your business and promise more than 150 types of rice dishes—not really surprising when almost all you can see for miles around you are rice paddies. ⏱ *2–4 hr. 20km/12. 5miles from Valencia, on the Albufera*

Birdwatching

L'Albufera is 'twitcher' heaven and a haven to over 300 species of birds who regularly visit, among them over 7,000 pairs of heron who come to breed on the reed-filled banks. There are ducks, coot, gulls, and sandpipers among many other species. One most satisfying success has been the breeding of the purple swamphen, now recently recovering here from near extinction on the Mediterranean coastline. The springs that replenish the waters of the lagoon make L'Albufera a crucial reserve for species that were in serious danger of extinction and are now unique to this area.

Paella & Mealtimes

Rice has been almost a staple in the diet of Valencians for centuries, since it was introduced to the area in the 15th century by the Moors. Of the many rice dishes available here, the traditional and favorite is Paella Valenciana, made with chicken and rabbit, garrofo beans (a large broad bean), kidney beans, and sometimes snails. It is said that in days gone by, when it was cooked at lunchtime in the paddies where the farmers were working, duck and water rat were the meat ingredients.

And the other 149 dishes? Well, among them there are Arroz Negro, black rice, made with squid and its ink; and Arroz Abanda, fish and seafood, with garlic mayonnaise. Then there is Paella de Mariscos, seafood, and Arroz al horno (rice in the oven) with pork, chickpeas, and Morcilla, a black sausage. Rice dishes are usually eaten at lunchtime.

Valencians eat often through the day and mealtimes take a bit of getting used to, lunch is rarely started before 2.30pm and dinner at around 9.30pm. If you order a Paella Valenciana, the best bit for the cognoscenti is the caramelized bottom, scraped off the pan and called socarrat. Delicious!

tourist bus from Plaza de la Reina or by car take the cv500.

3️⃣ Restaurante El Rek. At the edge of the village of El Palmar, this is one of the best known *arrocerías* and has been a firm favorite since the 1970s. It's always busy at weekends, but particularly so on Sundays, when half of Valencia seems to descend on the village to enjoy a typical Sunday lunch, which always seems to last until late afternoon. *C/ Pintor Marti 1.* ☎ *96-162-0297. $$$$.*

Valencia-style paella.

Fancy a Round of Golf?

If you like golf, the 18-hole El Saler golf course is outstanding, with wind conditions said to be on a par with Scottish courses. The 72-par course, voted second best in Europe by US magazine, *Golf World*, is in the grounds of the only Parador hotel close to Valencia, allowing you to stay and play at the same place. *Parador Luis Vives, Avda. de los Pinares, 151, El Saler.* ☎ 96-161-1186.

4 **kids** **Pinedo.** A bus ride out of the city gets you to Pinedo. The Mediterranean is to the west of L'Albufera, separated from it by a narrow strip of pine- and shrub-covered sand dunes. Surrounded by rice paddies, the beaches remain unspoiled and non-commercial. The beaches here are not as developed as La Malvarrosa. Pinedo is a small beach resort with a bar- and restaurant-lined promenade. The beaches here are spotlessly clean, safe, and sandy, and continue almost unbroken right down to Perelló and Cullera, a distance of some 17miles/27km. 🕑 *1 hr. 8km/5 miles from the city. Metrobus: Pinedo.*

5 **kids** **El Saler.** Heading towards El Saler you can see the dunes backed by pine trees. There are refreshing walks through these wooded areas. Like Pinedo, El Saler is an old-style seaside resort, very quiet and uncommercial—it is hard to believe that it is so close to such a big and vibrant city. It offers a few small hotels, some campsites, trailer parks, and some good bars and restaurants (although they tend to be smarter and more expensive than you would normally expect for beach restaurants) serving decent home cooking. El Saler and its neighboring villages are all well worth visiting for their beaches, which are backed by sand dunes and pine woods. In the dunes along this stretch of beaches are a fair number of excellent seafood restaurants. 🕑 *2–4 hr. 11km/6miles from Valencia, on the Albufera tourist bus from Plaza de la Reina or by car take the cv500 etc. Metrobus: El Saler.*

6 **Arrocería Duna.** The name says it all: a rice restaurant in the sand dunes right on the beach of El Saler. The specialty here is *arroces melosos* (soup-like rice dishes made with fish and seafood). They also do a particularly good salt-baked fish, always deliciously moist when you break through the thick salt crust. It is very romantic in high summer to eat here and watch the sea as the sun sets behind you. *Rambla del Talla Foc, Playa del Saler.* ☎ 96-183-0490. *$$$$.* ●

Naturist Beaches

If you are looking for naturist beaches—most beaches, by the way, are topless—there are two unofficial ones along here. One is between Pinedo and El Saler, and the other further south at a more remote location at La Devesa.

Dining Best Bets

Most Magnificent Mussels
★★ Bar Pilar $ *C/ Moro Zeit 13* (p 95)

Most Perfect Paella
★★ La Riua $$ *C/ del Rec, 79 (p 99)*

Best Budget Take Out
Pans & Co. *Everywhere*

Best People Watching
★ EL Generalife $$ *Plaza de la Virgen (p 97)*

Best Drag Show Dining Experience
★★★ Turangalila $$$$ *C/ del Mar 34* (p 100)

Best Foodie Heaven
★★★ El Ángel Azul, $$$$ *C/ Conde Altea 33 (p 96)*

Best Indian & Cocktails
★★★ Dhaba, $$$ *Plaza Don Juan de Villarrasa 6 (p 96)*

Best Described Lunch or Dinner
★★★ Tapa2, $$$ *C/ Cardá 6 (p 99)*

Best Italian with a Twist
★ Al Pomodoro $$ *C/ del Mar, 22* (p 94)

Best Regional Italian
★ Hosteria el Vizio, $$ *C/ Eugenia Vines 107 (p 97)*

Best Tapas & Wine
★★★ Casa Montaña $$$ *C/ José Benlliure, 69 (p 95)*

Best Indian
★ Baz $ *C/ Llano de Zaidia, 155* (p 95)

Best Seaside Dining
★★ Arroceria Duna $$$ *Playa del Saler (p 88)*

Best Romantic
★★★ Dalaii Lounge $$$$ *C/ Gascó Oliag, 6 (p 96)*

Best for Noisy Kids
★★ Tony Roma's $$$ *Plz Canovas 2.* (p 99)

Best Lebanese Food
★★★ Beirut, $$ *C/ Alta (p 52)*

Enjoy tapas at a Valencian terrace café.

Centro Histórico Dining

(i) Information

(⊠) Post Office

(M) Metro Station

0 ————— 1/4 mi

0 ————— 0.25 km

Rest of Valencia Dining

Ca' Sento **1**
Casa Montaña **2**
Cinquante Cinq **3**
Diablito **4**
El Ángel Azul **5**
Hosteriá el Vizio **6**
La Lonja del Pescado Frito **7**
La Malquerida **8**
Submarino **9**
Tony Roma's **10**

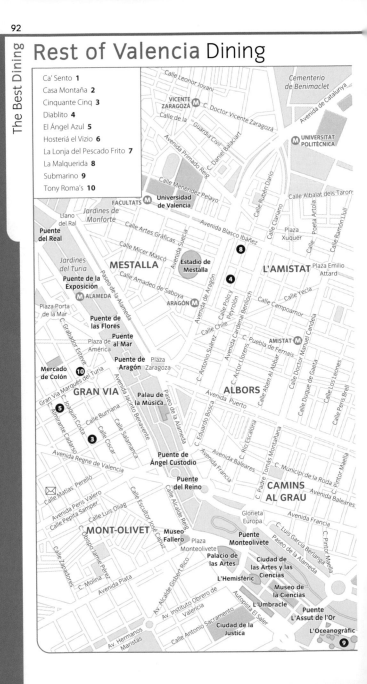

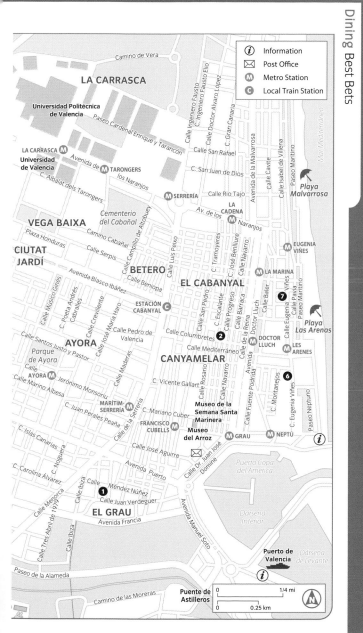

Camino de Vera

LA CARRASCA

Universidad Politécnica de Valencia

Paseo Cardenal Enrique y Tarancón

Calle Ingeniero Fausto

C. Ingeniero Fausto Elio

Calle Doctor Alvaro López

C. Gran Canaria

Calle San Rafael

LA CARRASCA Ⓜ

Universidad de Valencia

Avenida de Ⓜ **TARONGERS**

los Naranjos

C. Albalat dels Tarongers

C. San Juan de Dios

Ⓜ **SERRERÍA**

Calle Rio Tajo

Avenida de la Malvarrosa

Calle Cavite

Calle Isabel de Villena

Paseo Marítimo

Mar Mediterráneo

☂ Playa Malvarrosa

VEGA BAIXA

Plaza Honduras

CIUTAT JARDÍ

Cementerio del Cabañal

Camino Cabañal

Calle Serpis

Av. de los

LA CADENA Ⓜ

Naranjos

Avenida Blasco Ibáñez

BETERO

Calle Beniopa

Calle Campillo de Altobuey

Calle Luis Peixo

C. Tramoyeres

C. José Benlliure

Calle Navarro

Ⓜ **EUGENIA VIÑES**

Ⓜ **LA MARINA**

EL CABANYAL

Calle Baler

Calle Eugenia Viñes

Paseo Marítimo

Calle Pavía

☂ Playa Las Arenas

Calle Músico Ginés

Calle Poeta Andrés Cabrales

Calle Crevillente

Calle José María Haro

AYORA

Calle Santos Justo y Pastor

Parque de Ayora

Calle

AYORA Ⓜ

Calle Marino Albesa

Jerónimo Monsoriu

ESTACIÓN CABANYAL Ⓒ

Calle Pedro de Valencia

Calle Columbretes

Calle San Pedro

C. Escalante

Calle Progreso

Calle Barraca

Calle de la Reina

Ⓜ Doctor Lluch

❷

Calle Mediterráneo

Calle Rosario

CANYAMELAR

Calle Navarro

Avenida de la Serrería

DOCTOR LLUCH Ⓜ

LES ARENES Ⓜ

❻

C. Montanejos

C. Eugenia Viñes

Paseo Neptuno

Calle Maderas

C. Vicente Gallart

Calle Fuente Podrida

MARÍTIM-SERRERÍA Ⓜ

C. Juan Perales Peaña

C. Mariano Cuber

Museo de la Semana Santa Marinera

FRANCISCO CUBELLS Ⓜ

Museo del Arroz

Ⓜ **GRAU**

Ⓜ **NEPTÚ**

C. Islas Canarias

C. Noguera

Calle José Aguirre

⊠

ⓘ

Puerto Copa del América

C. Carolina Álvarez

Avenida Puerto

Calle Dr. Juan José Domine

Dársena Interior

Calle Tres Abril de 1979

Calle Menorca

Calle Ibiza

Calle

Méndez Núñez

❶

Calle Juan Verdeguer

EL GRAU

Avenida Francia

Avenida Manuel Soto

Puerto de Valencia 🚢

Dársena de Levante

Paseo de la Alameda

Camino de las Moreras

Puente de Astilleros

ⓘ

0 ——— 1/4 mi

0 ——— 0.25 km

Valencia Dining A to Z

kids 100 (Cien) Montaditos

CENTRO *SPANISH FAST FOOD*
A fun and cheap way to eat—small bread rolls are stuffed with the filling of your choice from more than 100 tapas-style fillings. Served on a wooden platter piled with potato chips and all for 1.15€, it makes for a very inexpensive snack or meal. Two rolls are ample, three or four if you are really hungry. *Plaza de la Reina 16 and various other addresses in the city.* ☎ *93-268-7017. Small rolls. 1.15€. Map p 91.*

★★ kids Al Pomodoro CENTRO

ITALIAN Our family favorite this one, we love the starters so much we tend to just stick to them. I suggest the mouthwatering tempura vegetables and the puffy pockets of bread with dipping sauces, followed by a couple of the paper-thin pizzas and the best tiramisu in town. Always book, especially at weekends. *C/ del Mar, 22.* ☎ *93-319-6600. Menú del Día 10€ Pizzas 8€–12€. AE, MC, V. Lunch 2–4pm, dinner 9–12pm. Map p 91.*

★ Babalu BARRIO DEL CARMEN

CUBAN/CARIBBEAN A Cuban/Caribbean restaurant and bar that offers flavors from around the world, billing itself as an original gastronomic and cultural adventure. The food is delicious and the portions generous, try the 12€ Tapas Caribeños (for two), a huge platter of delicacies. Mojitos and Caipirinhas are great value served by the jug. *C/ Manyans, 17.* ☎ *96-315-5040/66-629-8842. Entrees 8€–12€. Daily menu 13€. Tasting menu 18€. AE, DC, MC, V. Lunch & dinner daily. Bus: 5b, 7, 27, 28, 60, 81. Metro: Xàtiva. Map p 91.*

★ Bamboo CENTRO MEDITER-

RANEAN FUSION This cool and spacious restaurant is situated behind the glass waterfall in the basement of the gorgeous Mercado de Colón (see bullet ❸, p 43).

Al Pomodoro for top-notch tiramisu.

While their menu is described by them as 'eclectic fusion', I think it has its feet firmly in the Med: they offer a daily rice dish each lunchtime—and you can't get more Valencian than that. *Mercado de Colón C/ Jorge Juan,19.* ☎ 96-353-0337. *Entrees 12€–29€. Daily menu 12.95€. Tasting menu 35€. AE, DC, MC, V. Lunch & dinner daily. Bus: 2, 3, 4, 32, 79, 80, 81. Metro: Colón. Map p 91.*

★ **Bar Pilar** BARRIO DEL CARMEN *VALENCIAN* This place probably hasn't changed since it opened its doors more than 70 years ago. The selection of tapas is no different from any other bar but the specialty here is steamed mussels. Buckets line the bottom of the bar for the shells. Don't be surprised to find queues; it may look dingy, but it attracts an affluent crowd. *Moro Zeit, 27. Tapas 5€–6€. No credit cards. 12pm–midnight daily. Bus: 5b. Map p 91.*

Baz SAIDIA *INDIAN/PAKISTANI* At Baz, the Indian/Pakistani cuisine does a very good job of tingling the tastebuds—the tandoori and tikka served sizzling at your table are always good here. A little off the beaten track, but worth the effort. *C/ Llano de Zaidia, 155.* ☎ 61-723-3402. *Entrees 5€–9€; lunch 8€. AE, MC, V. Lunch & dinner daily. Bus: 95. Map p 91.*

★ kids **Boing Boing** CENTRO *FUSION* Have a drink at one of the snazzy bars in this three-floor mansion or choose from fabulous tempura prawns (to die for) or delicious mouth-size hamburgers with relish. All dishes are designed for sharing, *compartir* in Spanish. *C/ Conde Montornés, 8.* ☎ 96-392-0202. *Entrees 5€–15€. Around 25€ a head. www.momentosgustosos.com. AE, DC, MC, V. Lunch & dinner Mon–Fri. Bus: 31, 36, 70, 71. Map p 91.*

★★ **Burdeos in Love** CENTRO *MEDITERRANEAN FUSION* Sophisticated, modern and trendy, but with antique chandeliers and original architectural gems, it attracts the cool business set at lunchtime and romantic couples for dinner. Recommended dishes include an excellent shrimp ravioli and a good monkfish (rape). The wine list is extensive. *C/ del Mar.* ☎ 96-391-4350. *Entrees 12€–23€. Tasting menu 40€–50€. AE, DC, MC, V. Lunch & dinner Mon–Sat. Bus: 31, 36, 70, 71. Map p 91.*

★★ **Ca' Sento** PORT *MEDITERRANEAN* Ca' Sento has earned its young chef, Raul Alexandre, a well-deserved Michelin star. He specializes in Mediterranean cuisine, mainly fish and seafood, with a twist such as lobster with caramelized tomato. Essential to book. *C/ Méndez Núñez, 17.* ☎ 96-330-1775. *Entrees 30€–40€. Taster menu 70€. AE, DC, MC, V. Lunch & dinner Mon–Sat; Lunch Sun. Bus: 1, 2, 3, 4, 6, 19. Map p 92.*

★★★ **Casa Montaña** CABAÑAL *VALENCIAN* The tapas at this traditional bodega are delicious—you must try *croquettas de bacalao* (potato and cod fish cakes), and the divine *titaina* (a typical Cabañal dish of tuna, tomato, peppers, and pine nuts). Diners come here to appreciate the owner, Emiliano's vast knowledge of the food and wine industry. *C/ José Benlliure, 69.* ☎ 96-367-2314. *Tapas 5€–6€. AE, MC, V. Lunch & dinner Mon–Fri. Metro: Jaume I. Map p 92.*

★★ **Chust Godoy** BARRIO DEL CARMEN *CREATIVE VALENCIAN* Warm, intimate, and inviting, it's like eating in a friend's dining room. I always find it difficult to decide between their simply cooked meat or fish, as both are invariably superb. In the fall, try the 9-course hunting *degustación* (tasting) menu, of wild boar, venison, partridge, and pheasant. *C/ Boix, 6.* ☎ *96-391-3815. www.chustgodoy.com. Entrees 16€–25€. Taster menu 35€–50€. AE, DC, MC, V. Lunch & dinner Mon–Fri; Dinner Sat. Bus: 2, 80, 95. Map p 91.*

★ **Cinquante Cinq** CANÓVAS *FRENCH*   Alisdair Moore is, surprisingly, an Englishman, who runs an extremely successful French restaurant with verve. The confit de canard is sublime and the grilled tuna marinaded in lime and ginger is a favorite of ours. His menú del día at just 15€ is one of the best weekday deals in the city. *C/ Joaquín Costa 55.* ☎ *96-325-5029. Entrees 10€–20€. Taster menu 25€. Menú del Día 15€ and 25€. AE, DC, MC, V. Lunch & dinner Tues–Sat; Lunch Mon. Bus: 13, 17. Map p 92.*

★★ **Dalaii Lounge** CENTRO *CREATIVE VALENCIAN*   A romantic setting with flowing deep-colored nets. You can't go wrong with steak or fish accompanied by foie-gras and truffles, plum sauce, and caramelized onion, followed by homemade chocolate brownie and ice cream. Relax with coffee after your meal on cushions in the small chill area at the back. A short taxi ride from the city. *C/ Gascó Oliag, 6.* ☎ *96-336-9435. www.restaurantedalaii.com. Open Mon–Fri from 9am for breakfast, lunch & dinner; Fri and Sat dinner only. Entrees 12€–19€. Bus: 10, 12, 21, 29, 79, 89.*

★★ **Dhaba** CENTRO *INDIAN*   This smart, stylish and attractive cocktail bar restaurant serves authentic Indian food. At lunchtime they offer a sampler menu of *thalis* served on a tray with bread and a poppadom for only 14€ per head. *Plaza Don Juan de Villarrasa 6.* ☎ *96-391-0019. www.dhaba.es. Entrees 5€–12€; menú del día 14€. AE, DC, MC,*

El Generalife near the Plaza de la Virgen.

V. Lunch & dinner daily till midnight. Bus: 5b.

★★ **Diablito** ARAGÓN *MEXICAN-ITALIAN*   Fun, cool tribal interior and tasty food. This large and busy restaurant serves an unusual Italian-mixed-with-Mexican menu: fajitas and pizza, pasta and nachos. Diablito's has a funky bar/chill-out zone upstairs that is ideal for pre-dinner/club drinks to music from resident DJs. *C/ Polo y Peyrolon 57.* ☎ *96-328-8088. Entrees 8€–12€ AE, MC, V. Dinner daily till 1.30am. Bus: 32. Metro: Aragon.*

★★ **El Ángel Azul** CANOVAS *CREATIVE VALENCIAN*   The food and service are consistently good; the dining rooms are cozy and intimate, and there is always artwork by local artists on the walls. Specializing in market-fresh meats, fish, and vegetables, their food is always cooked to perfection and beautifully presented. One of my favorites is *lomo de buey* (ox filet pan-fried with bacon lardons), while my wife always chooses the monkfish. *C/ Conde Altea, 33.* ☎ *96-374-5656.*

www.restauranteelangelazul.com.
*Entrees 16€–24€; Tasting menu
40€. AE, DC, MC, V. Lunch & dinner
Tues–Sat. Bus: 13, 79, 80. Metro:
Colón. Map p 92.*

El Generalife BARRIO DEL CAR-
MEN *VALENCIAN SPANISH* Attractively laid and dressed tables sit on
the pavement, where diners can
watch the constant procession of
people in and out of Plaza de la
Virgen (see p 10, bullet **⑫**).
Fortunately, they produce very
good paellas, meat, and fish dishes
at a fair price, considering the
exceptional location. *C/ Caballeros 5.*
☎ *96-391-7899. Entrees 12€–18€;
menú del día 16€. AE, DC, MC, V.
Lunch & dinner Mon–Fri. Bus: 5, 5b.
Map p 91.*

★ **Hosteria el Vizio** MALVAR-
ROSA *REGIONAL ITALIAN* Excellent
meats such as mouthwatering rare
roast beef and gently marinaded
pork with delicate spices are among
my favorites on the menu. But I do
love the pasta dishes too—the
lasagne has to be one of the best in
Valencia—and their risottos are also

divine. There is a good terrace for
the warmer months. *C/ Eugenia
Vines 107.* ☎ *96-372-7778. www.
hosteriaelvizio.com. Entrees 8€–
14€; Tasting menu 40€. AE, DC, MC,
V. Open daily, all day until midnight.
Bus: 1, 2, 20, 22, 23. Tram: Dr Lluch,
Metro: Neptú. Map p 92.*

★ **La Champagne** CENTRO
FRENCH Sit under a huge picture
of the Eiffel Tower and enjoy some
of the city's very best French cuisine. Classic French dishes are perfectly cooked and presented, such
as melt-in-the-mouth duck à l'orange
or solomillo (filet) with foie gras
(interestingly, the Spanish just say
foie), which is mouthwateringly delicious. To finish? No contest, you just
have to order my favorite, tarte
tatin. *C/ Poeta Liern, 27.* ☎ *96-394-
2970. www.restaurantelachampagne.
com. Entrees 14€–25€. AE, DC, MC,
V. Lunch & dinner Tues–Sat. Metro:
Barceloneta. Map p 91.*

La Llantia Dorada CENTRO
INTERNATIONAL There's a dis-
tinctly Middle Eastern feel to this
tiny, intimate restaurant, just off the

French cuisine at La Champagne.

La Malquerida.

Plaza de la Virgen. Its purple walls and dimmed lighting from Moroccan lamps and candles set the mood. The menu is a mix of dishes from the Mediterranean, the Caribbean, and Asia. Expect anything from a smoky tandoori-style chicken salad to tagine or a Caribbean fish lasagne. *C/ Hierba 4 (off Plaza de la Virgen).* ☎ *96-391-2716. Entrees 8€–15€; tasting menu 16€ and 24€; menú del día 10€. AE, DC, MC, V. Lunch & dinner Mon–Fri; Dinner Sat. Bus: 5b, 95.*

La Lonja del Pescado Frito

CABANYAL *FISH* If the smell of fish frying doesn't bother you, or you miss your fish and chips from back home, then try this crazy fish restaurant. Eat the freshest fish and seafood at incredibly low prices, while dining among noisy locals. Hidden a road back from all the smarter restaurants, this is a must for choosy diners who don't want to spend a fortune. *C/ Eugenia Vines 243.* ☎ *96-355-3535. Entrees 5€–12€. Lunch & dinner Mon–Sat. Closed last 2 weeks in Aug. Metro: Neptú. Map p 92.*

★★ La Malquerida ARAGÓN

SPANISH The name La Malquerida, meaning the unloved, comes from an *amuse-bouche*, a secret passed on from generation to generation, that they serve between the starter and main course. Many of the dishes are tapas based—we started with Ibericos, delicious hams and cheeses and went on to eat one of the finest steaks I have had in a long while. *C/ Polo y Peyrolon, 53.* ☎ *96-389-1186. www.lamalquerida.com. Entrees 10€–22€; tasting menu 40€–55€; lunch 15€. AE, DC, MC, V. Lunch & dinner Mon–Fri & Sun; Dinner Sat. Bus: 32. Metro: Aragón. Map p 92.*

★ La Masía del Vino CENTRO

TRADITIONAL SPANISH A typical Spanish restaurant. It is huge but with a warm atmosphere and serves high quality tapas and food. Lunch is a bargain: three courses, wine, and bread for 12€. *C/ Hospital, 16* ☎ *96-392-1566. Menú del día 12€. Entrees 7€–16€. AE, DC, MC, V. 9am–5pm & 7.30–11.30pm Mon–Sat. Metro: Ángel Guimerà. Bus: 5b, 7, 13, 28, 60. Map p 91.*

★★ **La Riua** CENTRO *TRADITIONAL VALENCIAN* A particular favorite of Valencians, La Riua serves more than 15 rice dishes, paellas, and traditional Valencian cuisine. If you don't fancy their paellas, try *all i pebre* (stew made from eel, potato, garlic, and chili) and the wonderful *verduras a la plancha* (seasonal grilled vegetables) in which the globe artichokes are particularly scrumptious. If you don't want to wait at your table for up to an hour, call ahead and make your order. *C/ del Mar 27.* ☎ *96-391-9183. Paellas and rices from 12€. Entrees 13€–15€. AE, DC, MC, V. Lunch & dinner Mon–Sat. Bus: 31, 36, 70, 71. Map p 91.*

★★ **La Sucursal** CENTRO *MODERN VALENCIAN* La Sucursal—inside Valencia's Modern Art Museum IVAM— produces a modern twist on Valencian cuisine. Rice is a favorite here, but it is the caldoso (wet soupy) style—try the lobster (*bogavente*) caldoso. The rabbit loin (*lomo de conejo*) with artichokes and lemon thyme is also delicious. *C/ Guillém de Castro 118.* ☎ *96-374-6665. www.restaurante lasucursal.com. Entrees 25€, 30€, menu degustación 70€ . AE, DC, MC, V. Lunch Mon–Fri & dinner Mon–Sat. Metro:Túria. Bus: 5, 95. Map p 91.*

★ **Submarino** CIUDAD DE LES ARTES Y SCIENCIAS *MEDITERRANEAN FUSION* Down in the depths of the Oceanogràfic (you have to be escorted to the door in the evening) (see p 25, bullet ➐), surrounded by an immense aquarium with some ten thousand fish swimming around, some diners might feel a little hesitant to eat fish. The last time my wife and I ate here we opted for the delicious shoulder of lamb with puréed zucchini instead. The menu is quite eclectic, a mix of Mediterranean with some

Oriental twists. An extravagant setting. *Autopista El Saler 5.* ☎ *96-197-5565 and 902-100-131. Entrees 17€–30€, taster menu 60€. AE, MC, V. Lunch & dinner Mon–Sat; Lunch Sun. Bus: 35, 95. Map p 92.*

★★★ **Tapa2** CENTRO *MEDITERRANEAN FUSION* Two young Michelin-starred chefs, one English, Eddie, and the other German, Michael, set up this intimate restaurant with an open-plan kitchen. The food is exquisite and market-fresh and each dish is presented as a work of art. Their crisp praline of bull's tail with a chupito of pineapple and basil is to die for, and who would have thought of combining grilled calamari and black sausage (*morcilla*) with a sweet apple sauce? *C/ Cardá, 6.* ☎ *96-392-1470. tapa2 gastronomik.com. Entrees 8€–18€, taster menu 60€. AE, MC, V. Lunch & dinner Mon–Sat. Bus: 7, 60, 81.*

★ **kids** **Tony Roma's** CANÓVAS *AMERICAN* Life is not worth living without the occasional hamburger, and in Valencia it just has to be Tony Roma's, a little corner of USA in

Piano bar at the Submarino.

Locals snack on horchata y fartons.

Valencia. Order the combo and you are in for a feast—their famous and delicious ribs, an onion ring pile, gooey BBQ chicken, and all the trimmings. *Plaza Canovas, 2.* ☎ *96-351-3433. Entrees 8€–20€; fixed-price lunch menu 14€. AE, DC, MC, V. Lunch & dinner daily. Bus: 1, 13, 22, 41, 79. Map p 92.*

Turangalila CENTRO *MEDITER-RANEAN* Enjoy a lively floorshow with drag queens and comedy while you tuck into three excellent courses in the outrageous surroundings of this restaurant. A fun evening for couples and small groups, but booking is a must. At lunchtime they serve a lower-priced menu del día—without the show, unfortunately. *C/ del Mar, 34.* ☎ *96-391-0255.*

Dinner & show 25€–30€; menú del día 12€. MC, V. Lunch & dinner Mon–Fri; Dinner Sat. Bus: 31, 36, 70, 71. Map p 91.

★ **Yuso** BARRIO DEL CARMEN *RIOJA* Hidden in the backstreets near Calle Serranos, this earthy restaurant serves tapas and rice dishes typical of the famous La Rioja region. My favorite tapa is their *patatas yuso*, crispy slices of potato, scrambled egg, *morcilla* (black pudding) and a secret mix of herbs. I also like their *arroces melosos*, best described as soupy rices. *C/ Cruz 4.* ☎ *96-315-3967. Entrees 9€–13€; rices from 9€; menus 10€. AE, DC, MC, V. Lunch & dinner Tues–Sat; Lunch Sun. Bus: 5, 5b. Map p 91.* ●

Nightlife Best Bets

Fountain at night, Plaza de la Virgen.

Best Hipster Hangout
★★ The Mill Clubs, *C/ Padre Porta, 2* (p 109)

Best for Hardcore Clubbers
★★★ Barraca, *C/ Les Palmeres (Sueca)* (p 108)

Best Summer Night
★★★ Las Animas Puerto, *C/ Dr. Marcos Sapena, 52* (p 109)

Best Shimmy with a Shark
La Indiana, *C/ San Vicente, 95* (p 109)

Best Traditional Valencian Night Out
★★ Café Madrid, *C/ Abadia San Martín, 10* (p 105)

Best Celeb Haunt
★ Pacha, *C/ San Vicente, 305* (p 110)

Best Club in an Old House
★★★ Calcata, *C/ Reloj Viejo, 6* (p 108)

Best Seen and Be Seen Scene
★★★ On The Rocks, *Paseo Alameda, 45* (p 107)

Best Cocktails
★★ Marrasquino, *Plaza Doctor Andreu, 2* (p 107)

Best for People Watching
★ La Infanta, *Plaza Tossal, 3-4* (p 107)

Best Irish Pub
St Patrick's, *Gran Via Marqués Del Túria, 69* (p 108)

Best Jazz Bar
★★ Jimmy Glass Jazz Pub, *C/ Baja, 28* (p 111)

Best After Hours
★★★ 39°27N, *Cami d'en Corts, 54* (p 105)

Best for Salsa Aficionados
★★ Johnny Maracas, *C/ Caballeros, 39* (p 107)

Best Eclectic
★★★ Radio City, *C/ Santa Teresa,19* (p 108)

Best Reggae
★★ Dub Club, *C/ Jesús, 91* (p 109)

Best Beach Café
★ Café del Mar, *Paseo Maritimo de la Malvarrosa, Módulo nº8* (p 111)

Beach Nightlife

1 39º 27N
2 Barraca
3 Café del Mar
4 Estrella Damm Bar
5 Gandhara
6 Las Animas Puerto
7 The Mill Clubs

Calle San Juan de Dios
C. Doctor Álvaro López
Hospital San Juan De Dios
Calle Río Tajo
Avenida de la Malvarrosa
Calle Cavite
C. Isabel de Villena
Calle Pavía
Paseo Marítimo
Playa Malvarrosa

Av. de los Naranjos
LA CADENA
Hospital Malvarrosa
Mar Mediterráneo

Calle Remonta
C. Actor Mauri
C. Campillo de Altobuey
Calle Antonio
Calle Luis Peixo
Calle Ramón Rocafull
C. Pedro Maza
C. Tramoyeres
Calle Escalante
C. José Benlliure
Calle Navarro
Calle de la Reina
Doctor Lluch
EUGENIA VIÑES
LA MARINA
Calle Pintor
Avenida Ferrandis
GANDHARA
Juan

BETERO
Calle Beniopa
Calle Vicente Blasco Ibáñez
Calle Cura Planells
Calle Baler
Calle Eugenia Viñes
Paseo Marítimo
Playa Las Arenas

Avenida Blasco Ibáñez
EL CABANYAL
ESTACIÓN CABANYAL
Calle Mijares
Calle San Pedro
Calle Escalante
Calle Progreso
Calle Barraca
C. Pescadores

Calle Pedro de Valencia
Calle Columbretes
DOCTOR LLUCH
LES ARENES

Calle Maderas
Calle Mediterráneo
CANYAMELAR
Calle Mediterráneo
Calle Virgen del Sufragio

C. Arquitecto Alfaro
Serrería
C. Ernesto Anastasio
C. Francisco Baldoma
Calle Vicente
Calle Vicente Gallart
Calle Brull
Calle Rosario
Calle Navarro
Calle de la Reina
Avenida Doctor Lluch
Calle Fuente Podrida
Calle Arzobispo Guanduxe
Calle Montán
Calle Montanejos
Calle Eugenia Viñes
Paseo Neptuno

MARÍTIM-SERRERÍA
Calle Mariano Cuber
FRANCISCO CUBELLS
Museo de la Semana Santa Marinera
Museo del Arroz
Reales Atarazanas
GRAU
NEPTÚ
Calle Dr.
Marcos Sopena

Calle de la
Calle Consuelo
Calle José Aguirre
Calle Doctor Juan José Domine
Puerto Copa del América

The Mill Clubs
Avenida Puerto
Calle Vidal de Balnes
C. Méndez Núñez
Calle Bello
Calle Juan José Síster
Avenida Manuel Soto
Dársena Interior

(i) Information
✉ Post Office
Ⓜ Metro Station
Ⓒ Local Train Station

0   1/4 mi
0   0.25 km

Centro Histórico Nightlife

Black Note **1**
Café Carioca **2**
Café de las Horas **3**
Café de la Seu **4**
Café Madrid **5**
Café Valencia **6**
Calcata **7**
Deseo 54 **8**
Dub Club **9**
El Horno de los Borrachos **10**
El Loco **11**
El Mosquito **12**
Femme Fatale **13**
Flow **14**
Fox Congo **15**
Hoss **16**
Ishaya **17**
Jimmy Glass Jazz Pub **18**
Johnny Maracas **19**
La Indiana **20**
La Infanta **21**
M.Y.A / L'Umbracle **22**
Marrasquino **23**
Mirror **24**
On the Rocks **25**
Pacha Valencia **26**
Radio City **27**
Saint Patrick's Irish Bar **28**
Sally O'Brien **29**
Treinta y Tantos **30**

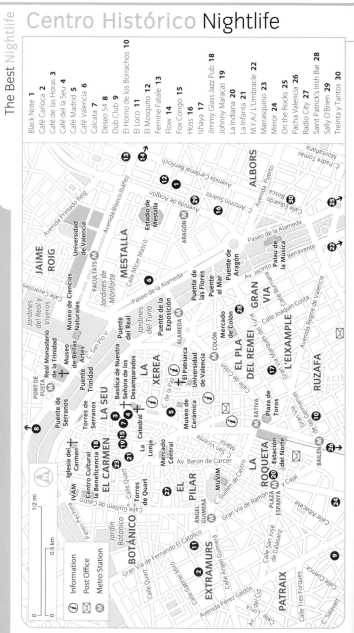

Valencia Nightlife A to Z

Bars & Pubs

★ **39°27N** MARINA REAL JUAN CARLOS   Stark white lines and designed almost completely with glass, this is a very chilled chillout bar with views across the marina to one side and Malvarrosa beach to the other. There is a small and very good dining area. This is the perfect place to watch the sailing during the day and to stop for dinner and pre-clubbing drinks at night. The atmosphere is super cool and it opens until the very early hours. *Marina Real Juan Carlos I, Port America's Cup.* ☎ *96-381-7171. Metro: Neptú. Map p 103.*

★ **Café Carioca** JUAN LLORENS Definitely not a 'karaoke' bar! This, one of the oldest clubs in Valencia, guarantees a fun night out in a quirkily decorated bar with tiny mirrors and lots of ripply plasterwork. As with most clubs, all ages are welcome, but here it is even more apparent. Most nights there is a good selection of pop music to dance to as well as themed music nights: R'n'B, country and western, and electronic. *C/ Juan Lorens 48.*

The chill bar at 39°27N.

Bus: 3, 17, 70, 72. Metro: Angel Guimerà. Map p 104.

★★ **Café de las Horas** BARRIO DEL CARMEN   Just off the Plaza de la Virgen, this truly decadent bar and café is well worth a visit—the walls are decorated right up to the high ceilings with all sorts of antiques and ephemera. Perfect for an intimate cappuccino, pre-dinner aperitifs, or post-dinner digestifs with friends. *C/ Tallers, 1.* ☎ *93-318-8826. Bus: 5b. Map p 104.*

★★★ **Café Madrid** CENTRO   All gilt frames and burgundy walls, with its bars on different levels and unique booths in nooks and crannies Café Madrid is a haven for smart Valencian businessmen and women to relax with some Agua de Valencia after a hard day at work. Take care though, Aqua de Valencia is a strong mix of Cava, spirits, and orange juice, and can take its toll very quickly. *C/ Abadía San Martin, 10.* ☎ *96-385-0330. Bus: 4, 6, 8, 9, 11. Map p 104.*

★★ **Café Valencia** ALAMEDA Between Puente de las Flores and

Puente de la Reina, this leafy avenue of the Alameda is packed with bars, their terraces under the trees in the middle. Expect Ralph Lauren polos, smart shirts with jeans, and ultra-polished, fashionable ladies. Café Valencia is a staple for a summer afternoon in the shade or to kick off an evening out. *Paseo de la Alameda, 14.* ☎ *96-369-3262. Bus: 1, 11, 70, N1, N2, N3. Metro: Alameda. Map p 104.*

★ **El Mosquito** ARAGÓN   A favorite of a more classic, laid-back crowd. I especially love the collection of clocks, behind the bar, with international times (including Tokyo and the nearby Valencian town of Bétera) and the giant hanging papier-mâché mosquito. Excellent for house, funk, and soul and for picking up flyers and VIP tickets for all the hot clubs. *C/ Polo y Peyrolón, 11. No phone. Metro: Aragón. Map p 104.*

★ **Flow** PLAZA HONDURAS   For those that like their irregular beats and kooky crowds, this galley-like bar, right in the middle of the student area of town near the university faculties, is a must for its drum'n'bass, '50s rock, and breakbeat. *Plaza de Honduras 35.* ☎ *93-318-7980. www.myspace. com/flowvalencia. Metro: Aragón. Map p 104.*

★★★ **Fox Congo** BARRIO DEL CARMEN   House music, Brazilian nights, and hip-hop Wednesdays make up the weekly timetable at this Carmen staple. There is a good mix of people and a very interna-tional crowd. The leather-clad walls, dim lighting, and leafy interior in the toilets are all plus points, too. *C/ Caballeros, 35.* ☎ *96-392-5527. Bus: 5, 5b. Map p 104.*

★ **Hoss** ARAGÓN   With state-of-the-art video performances, the best Valencian DJs at the decks, and amazing murals on the walls, this is a super cool bar with friendly staff. Popular with a trendy young crowd. *C/ Eolo, 18. No phone. Metro: Aragón. Map p 104.*

Valencia by Night : What's Cod Got to Do With It?

The nightlife in Valencia is renowned for being the best in main-land Spain. Back in the 1980s, the Movida Valenciana (a massive movement of New-Wave groups influenced by the likes of Soft Cell and Bowie), brought hundreds of young Spaniards in droves to the area from Madrid and Barcelona on a Friday evening, partying hard all the way through to Monday morning before going back to work. This phenomenon, named La Ruta del Bacalao (literally translated, Cod Route), lasted until the mid-1990s, and firmly established Valen-cia as Spain's clubbing capital. Things start rolling around 11.30pm after a late lazy dinner, with the bars and pubs closing from 1.30am to 3.30am and the clubs staying open until at least 6.30am. Most bars have free entry (though some make males pay) and clubs charge anything from 8 to 20€ on the door, but 12€ or 15€ is aver-age, and usually includes a free drink. Be warned—Valencians are extremely generous with their measures.

Café de las Horas.

★★★ **Ishaya** GRAN VÍA MARQUÉS DEL TÚRIA (CÁNOVAS) The Las Animas group is famous in the city for having the most up-market establishments, and Ishaya is no exception. This luxurious and elegant Buddha-themed lounge bar has a strict door policy and employs only beautiful staff to match its interior. It attracts a slightly older, impeccably dressed crowd. Expect higher prices on drinks but an exclusive evening out. *Gran Vía Marqués del Túria, 23. Group Number ☎ 90-210-8527. www.grupolasanimas.com. Metro: Colón. Bus: 1, 13, 41, 49, 72, 80. Map p 104.*

★★ **Johnny Maracas** BARRIO DEL CARMEN If you like salsa dancing, this is the place to be. Latin sounds pump out of the speakers from Wednesday to Sunday nights, and often live Latin acts play for a friendly and energetic crowd. *C/ Caballeros 39. ☎ 96-391-5266. Bus: 5, 5b. Map p 104.*

★★ **La Infanta** BARRIO DEL CARMEN The Plaza del Tossal is a central meeting point in the Barrio del Carmen, and the flux of people through the square is constant. Hide out inside La Infanta in the delicately beautiful 1950s' movie-star inspired interior or sit out on the large terrace and watch the world go by. *Plaza del Tossal 3–4. ☎ 96-392-1623. Bus: 5b. Map p 104.*

★★★ **Marrasquino** BARRIO DEL CARMEN Also in the Plaza del Tossal, Marrasquino is highly popular—sometimes I've had to leave for want of elbowroom. The DJ upstairs rocks out pumping house music and downstairs at the bar you can choose from one of the most extensive cocktail lists in the city. Their mojitos are particularly delicious and can be enjoyed outside in the warmer months. *Plaza San Jaime, 1. ☎ 96-391-6427. Bus: 5, 5b, 28. Map p 104.*

★★ **On the Rocks** ALAMEDA One of the bars that popped up in time for the America's Cup elite to enjoy, but is here to stay. Gorgeous people are surrounded by a beautiful and unique décor, making this the perfect place to start your night out if dressed up to the nines. We recommend carrying on the party just over the road at M.Y.A. (see p 112), in the City of Arts and

On the Rocks.

Sciences. *Paseo de la Alameda, 45.*
☎ *96-381-4330. Bus: 19, 20, 40.*
Map p 104.

★★ **Radio City** BARRIO DEL CAR-
MEN   A night out in El Carmen
would not be complete without a
visit to Radio City. You're guaranteed a lively time here any night of
the week, they have kept the true
essence of the bar and the *barrio*
(neighborhood) alive with the most
eclectic crowd and program in
town. The music is a super-fun mix
of reggae, electro, punk, gospel,
garage—you name it. Don't forget
to look up at the ceilings at the front
of the bar: portraits of favorite faces
of Radio City are painted here. Grab
flyers here for the sister nightclub
Disco City. *C/ Santa Teresa, 19.*
☎ *96-391-4151. www.radiocity*
valencia.com. Bus: 5b. Map p 104.

★★★ **Saint Patrick's Irish Bar**
CÁNOVAS   Serving Guinness and
Murphy's on tap, this traditional
Irish bar prides itself on its warm
welcome to visitors and residents
alike. Mingle with a European mix of
punters, and don't forget they show
most league football matches as
well as important rugby, cricket, and
snooker on one or all of their four
plasma screens. *Gran Vía Marqués*
del Túria, 69. www.stpatricks
valencia.com. Metro: Colón. Bus: 1,
3, 15, 22, 41, 79, 80, N1. Map p 104.

★ **Sally O'Brien** ARAGÓN   A
Victorian-style Irish pub at the start
of the party area that is Aragón. Stop
by for a quick pint of Guinness or sit
and enjoy their whisky and cream
coffees. They often have live music
too, and surprisingly, for an Irish bar,
it attracts a mainly Spanish crowd.
Avda. Aragón, 8. ☎ *96-337-4012.*
Metro: Aragón. Map p 104.

Dance Clubs

★★★ **Barraca** SUECA   Quite a
way out of the city, but well worth
the taxi-ride if you are into your hard-
house and techno, this is one of the
original clubs from the 70s, 80s, and
90s that formed part of the infamous
Ruta del Bacalao—and still packs the
floor every weekend. A bus service
operates from the city (Cánovas and
Centro Comercial El Saler, by the City
of Arts and Sciences) too; check out
their website for more details. *C/ Les*
Palmeres (Sueca) No phone. www.
barracamusic.com. Admission
varies—look for flyers. Bus: there is a
special Barraca bus from Valencia,
cost 2€). Map p 103.

★★ **Calcata** BARRIO DEL CARMEN
One of the very few nightclubs in
the Carmen area in an authentic
15th-century Valencian building. All
three floors wrap around and look
down onto the central dancefloor in
the interior patio. There is a unique
card system on the door and a fun,

crowd-pleasing mix of music. The DJ is usually open to requests—a rare find. *C/ Reloj Viejo 6. Cover: minimum 8€. Bus: 5, 5b, 28, 80, 95. Map p 104.*

★★ **Dub Club** EXTRAMURS Dub Club is the place to be for reggae, hip-hop, funk, and breakbeat lovers. Check out their website for their concert, jam sessions, *café teatro*, and DJ-packed monthly program. *C/ Jesús, 91. www.dubclubvalencia.com. No cover. Metro: Jesús. Map p 104.*

★★★ **La Indiana** PLAZA ESPAÑA Having recently undergone a massive refurbishment (it almost burnt to the ground the day before New Year's Eve in 2007), this club is back with a bang. It was famous for its shark-filled aquaria before the fire, now it's the music. Three rooms offer different styles—house, funk, and latin—a superb music system, and a buzzing crowd. *C/ San Vicente, 95. ☎ 96-384-5051. www.laindiana.com. Cover: minimum 12€. Metro: Plaza de España. Map p 104.*

★★★ **Las Animas Puerto** PUERTO This place takes your breath away, it is one of the most stunning nightclubs in the city—

owned by the same people as Ishaya (see p 107). Expect breathtakingly high metal stairs up through the inside of the building, surrounded by Buddhas and candelabras, and once again, beautiful people. There are two huge decked areas upstairs, one pumping out some of the best house and electro, and the other playing Pechanga, what you might call cheesy Spanish pop—but great fun to dance to. Downstairs, the 'Dockas' part of the club is open all year round. *C/ Dr. Marcos Sapena, 52. Group Number ☎ 90-210-8527. www.grupolas animas.com. Cover 20€. Bus: 20, 22, 23. Metro: Neptú. Map p 103.*

★★★ **Mirror** ARRANCAPINS This club is enormous, and even when it's absolutely packed there is still room to breathe, dance, and more. The club has passed through various hands in the past few years but Mirror looks like it's here to stay. It has maintained the tradition of bringing big live acts to town on a regular basis. *C/ San Vicente, 200. www.discomirror.es. Cover: minimum 10€. Metro: Plaza de España. Map p 104.*

Busy café on Plaza de la Reina.

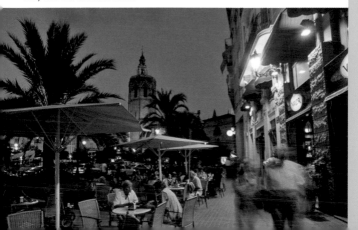

★★ **Pacha Valencia** CRUZ CUBIERTA   For die-hard Ibiza fans, a visit to Pacha will be a top priority while in the city. With two rooms, an incredible VIP area overlooking the whole dancefloor, and a no-expenses-spared décor, Pacha Valencia lives up to the club's legacy. The sound system is amazing, and Saturday nights are best. *C/ San Vicente, 305.* ☎ *63-977-4293. www.pachavalencia.com. Cover 20€. Bus: 27, N6. Map p 104.*

★★★ **The Mill Clubs** PUERTO The Groovelives group has bars and clubs all over the city, all offering something a little different. This one has three rooms: Teatro Stage, Freestyle Room, and The Factory. One ticket will let you roam and boogie through all three rooms to the sounds of techno, Indie, electro, punk, house, rock, soul, hip-hop, disco and more. Make sure you skimp on clothing—it can get hot in there! *C/ Padre Porta (Avda.Puerto). No phone. www.themillclubs.com. Cover 8€–10€. Bus: 2, 3, 4, 19, 20, 22, 30, N8. Map p 103.*

★★ **Treinta y Tantos** CIUDAD DE LAS ARTES Y LAS CIENCIAS   Due to the student clubbing scene being so big, this club has been welcomed with open arms by an older crowd of Valencian groovers—some nights the queues wrap around the block. Literally meaning "Thirty Somethings" this is an enjoyable spot for those who fancy a good old boogie on a Friday or Saturday night. *C/ Eduardo Boscá, 27.* ☎ *60-765-9705. www. 30itantos.es. Cover 15€. Bus: 19, 20, 40. Map p 104.*

Gay & Lesbian Bars/Clubs

★ **Café del la Seu** EL BARRIO DEL CARMEN   A little coffee shop with local art adorning the walls, though like every bar in Spain it sells the harder stuff, too. This is *the* gay meeting place. On a side street behind Plaza de la Virgen, they also have tables outside on a quiet pedestrian street. Their teas are delicious and always served with a few biscuits on the side. *C/ Santo Cáliz 7.* ☎ *96-391-5715. Bus: 4, 6, 8, 9, 11, 16. Map p 104.*

★★ **Deseo 54** LA SAIDIA   The most popular gay club in the city, a 5-minute walk from the Barrio del Carmen, the crowd is made up of all ages and types, from rough and rugged to pretty and preened, who come here either to cruise or in groups of friends to have a good time. The music is house and electro all the way, except for Thursdays, when Los Padres de Lola spin a groovy mix of old and new Spanish and international pop. *C/ Pepita, 15. No phone. www.deseo54.com. Cover: free before 3am on Fridays with a flyer, 10€–12€. Bus: 5b. Map p 104.*

★**Femme Fatale** XUQUÉR Strictly girls only, this lesbian bar is a really nice, trendy, friendly place to hang out. They often have themed parties and fun evenings for gals, and show movies and TV series on their large screen. *C/ Historiador Claudio Sanchez Albornoz, 6. Metro: Blasco Ibañez. Map p 104.*

Live Music

★★**Black Note** ARAGÓN   Ten years old, with more than 2,000 concerts under its belt, Black Note's jam sessions are mesmerizing fun to watch, and the set up is perfect to sit back at tables and watch whatever's happening on-stage. From 10pm to 3.30am every night this club has live music on the cards, from Flamenco to jazz to fusion and funky. *C/ Polo y Peyrolón,15. www. blacknoteclub.com. Most nights free except when there's a big name when prices vary. Metro: Aragón. Map p 104.*

The terrace at L'Umbracle.

★★**El Loco** JUAN LLORENS   Apart from the nationally famous groups that this club brings to town, I especially love the new acts nights around once a month, when Valencian groups hit the stage and there is a vote at the end of the evening. The vote, however, is by show of hands, so it's 'whoever brings the most friends' wins. *C/ Erudito Orellana, 12.* ☎ *96-392-2607. www.loco club.org. Cover: minimum 8€ but depends on the live act. Metro: Ángel Guimerà. Map p 104.*

★★★**Jimmy Glass Jazz Pub** EL BARRIO DEL CARMEN   Dark, smoky, ambient—you could be forgiven for thinking you were in a jazz bar in New York. With live acts on stage on a regular basis, you should stop by this authentic bar to enjoy blues, vocal jazz, and bebop in a seriously cool environment. *C/ Baja, 28. www.jimmyglassjazz.net. No phone. Cover: 4€–7€. Bus: 5b. Map p 104.*

Post-Clubbing Hangout
★ **El Horno de los Borrachos** RUZAFA   Literally the 'Bakery of the Drunks', this place opens through the night specifically to feed the up-all-nighters: party and club-goers, night and late-shift

workers. Now you know where to go when you're suffering from 'night starvation'. *C/ Sueca, 3.* ☎ *96-341-4920. www.elhornodelosborrachos. com. Bus: 1, 3, 19, 22, 40, 41.*

Summer Nights
★★ **Café del Mar** MALVARROSA   A franchise of the world-famous José Padilla-run original sunset chill bar in Ibiza, it has maintained all the authentic Café del Mar details, from the 1920s figurines to the fantastic draped ceiling in the dining area. Stay outside on the terrace as day falls into night with a cool beer, cocktail, or one of the wines from their extensive list. They also do lunches midweek that are a real bargain. Café del Mar is right on the seafront looking over the beach with live DJs playing chill-out tracks all day. *Paseo Marítimo de la Malvarrosa, Módulo nº8.* ☎ *96-355-6327. www.cafedelmarmusic.com. No cover. Bus: 20, 21, 22, 23, 32. Metro: Eugenia Viñes. Map p 103.*

★★★ **Estrella Damm Bar** PUERTO   Right on the dock of the port looking over the water of the marina, this bar was built for the America's Cup and has attracted such a following that it's still packed most summer evenings. It stays

Alameda terrace for summer nights.

open until 4am, and there are always live DJs on deck. You can take the Estrella Damm vibe home with you; their CD is on sale at the bar. *Marina Juan Carlos I, opposite Veles e Vents building. No phone. No cover. www.estrelladammlounge. com. Metro: Neptú. Map p 103.*

★★★ **Gandhara** MALVARROSA A lot of the summer clubs and *terrazas* (terraces) opt for a very spiritual theme when it comes to decoration—I like Gandhara's the most. From midnight on, every day of the week, you can enjoy either the small dance floor in the front of the club or, once through to the back, the gorgeous, Hindu art-inspired, open-air, chill-out style seating area, fab cocktail bar, and lush VIP sofas. Saris are used as curtains for a little privacy. It's a little known fact, but there are also shishas with fragrant tobacco available for use; they need to be

booked in advance. *C/ Eugenia Viñes 226.* ☎ *96-371-0025. www.gandhara terraza.com Cover 10€–15€. Metro: Eugenia Viñes (Tram). Map p 103.*

★★★ **M.Y.A./ L'Umbracle** CIUDAD DE LAS ARTES Y LAS CIENCIAS The spectacular surroundings of the City of Arts and Sciences provide the backdrop for this luxe summer terrace. Downstairs is the circular club M.Y.A., with a stage above the bar for live acts and a smart VIP area for all to see. L'Umbracle runs halfway along the ribcage-like structure, of the same name, opposite the Science Museum, and is a special place to chill out after dark on hot summer nights. You can even cash in your taxi fare with a receipt at the bar. *Autopista El Saler 1 (Ciudad de las Artes y las Ciencias).* ☎ *96-331-9745. www.umbracle terraza.com. Cover (except for special concerts) 12€. Bus: 35, 95. Map p 104.* ●

Arts & Entertainment Best Bets

Best Concert Hall
★ Palau de la Mùsica, *Paseo de la Alameda (p 117)*

Best Jazz Club
★ Black Note Club, *C/ Polo y Peyloron 15 (p 118)*

Best Flamenco
★★ Café del Duende, *C/ Túria 62 (p 118)*

Best Opera House
★★★ Palau de les Arts Reina Sofia, *Ciudad de las Artes y las Ciencias (p 118)*

Best Summer Concert Venue
★★ Jardines de Viveros, Feria de Julio *Jardines de Viveros (p 33)*

Best Sporting Event
★ Formula One European Grand Prix, *Marina Juan Carlos (p 119)*

Best Theater Performances
★ Teatro Principal, *C/ Barcus 15 (p 121)*

Best Bets
★ Gran Casino Monte Picayo, *Puzol (p 117)*

Best Sailing
★★ Marina Juan Carlos I, *Puerto de Valencia (p 120)*

Best Fire & Fireworks Fiesta in Spain
★★★ Las Fallas, *throughout the city and more (p 122)*

Best Summer Rock Festival
★ Festival Internacional de Benicàssim, *Benicàssim (p 157)*

Best Food Fight in the Entire World
★★ La Tomatina, *Buñol (p 157)*

Best Moviehouse for Original Version Films
UGC CINÉ CITÉ, *Avda. Tirso de Molina 16 (p 117)*

Mascletàs set up during Las Fallas.

Valencia A&E

Café del Duende **1**
Estadi Ciutat de València **2**
Estadi Nou Mestalla **3**
Gran Casino Monte Picayo **4**
IVAC Filmoteca **5**
Jimmy Glass Jazz Pub **6**
La Claca **7**
Las Fallas **8**
Radio City **9**
Teatro Olympia **10**
Teatro Principal **11**
Teatro Talia **12**
Trinquete Pelayo **13**
UGC CINÉ CITÉ **14**

(i) Information
✉ Post Office
Ⓜ Metro Station

0 _____ 1/4 mi
0 _____ 0.25 km

Beach A&E

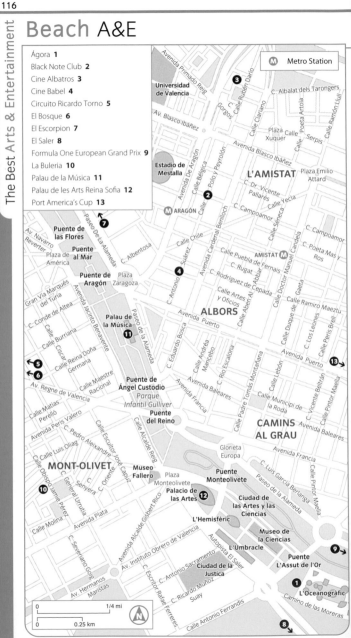

Ágora **1**
Black Note Club **2**
Cine Albatros **3**
Cine Babel **4**
Circuito Ricardo Torno **5**
El Bosque **6**
El Escorpion **7**
El Saler **8**
Formula One European Grand Prix **9**
La Buleria **10**
Palau de la Música **11**
Palau de les Arts Reina Sofia **12**
Port America's Cup **13**

Ⓜ Metro Station

Avenida Primado Reig
Universidad de Valencia
C. Albalat dels Tarongers
C. gorgos
Calle Rubén Darío
Calle Clariano
C. Ramón Llull
Av. Blasco Ibáñez
Calle Poeta Artola
Plaza Calle
Xuquer
Serpis
Avenida Blasco Ibáñez
Estadio de
Mestalla
Paseo De la Alameda
Calle Bélgica
L'AMISTAT
Plaza Emilio
Attard
Avenida De Aragón
Calle Polo y Peyrolón
C. Dr. Vicente
Pallarés
Calle Yecla
Calle Campoamor
C. Campoamor
Ⓜ ARAGÓN
Calle
Calle Cardenal Benlloch
Calle Seneca
C. Poeta Mas y
Ros
Puente de
las Flores
Calle Chile
AMISTAT Ⓜ
Av. Navarro
Reverter
C. Albentosa
Calle Puebla de Fernais
Puente
al Mar
C. Rugat
Calle Doctor Manuel Candela
Plaza de
América
Calle Antonio Suárez
Calle Rodriguez de Cepeda
Calle Gaeta
Puente de
Aragón
Plaza
Zaragoza
Calle Artes
y Oficios
Calle Aben Al Abbar
Calle Ramiro Maeztu
ALBORS
Palau de
la Música
Avenida Puerto
Calle Duque de Gaeta
Gran Vía Marqués
del Turia
C. Conde de Altea
C. Eduardo Bosca
Calle Andrés
Mancebo
C. Los Leones
Avenida Jacinto Benavente
Calle Burriana
Calle Cister
Calle Reina Doña
Germana
Paseo de la Alameda
C. Río Escalona
Avenida Puerto
Calle Peris Brell
Puente de
Ángel Custodio
Av. Regne de Valencia
Calle Maestre
Racional
Parque
Infantil Gulliver
Avenida Balears
Calle Lebón
Calle Municipi de
la Roda
Calle Matías
Perelló
Puente
del Reino
Avenida Francia
Calle Padre Tomás Montañana
CAMINS
AL GRAU
Avenida Peris Valero
C. Pedro Alexandre
Calle Escultor José Capuz
Calle Alcalde Reig
CAMINS
Avenida Balears
Calle Luis Oliag
Calle
Senyera
C. Oriente
Glorieta
Europa
Avenida Francia
Calle Vicente Beltrán
Calle Pintor Maella
MONT-OLIVET
Museo
Fallero
Plaza
Monteolivete
Puente
Monteolivete
C. Luis García Berlanga
Paseo de la Alameda
Calle Obispo Jaime Pérez
C. General Urrutia
Palacio de
las Artes
Ciudad de
las Artes y las
Ciencias
Calle Pintor Maella
Calle Molina
Avenida Plata
L'Hemisfèric
Museo de
la Ciencias
Avenida Alcalde Gisbert Rico
L'Umbracle
Av. Instituto Obrero de Valencia
Autopista El Saler
Puente
L'Assut de l'Or
C. Severiano Goig
Escritor Rafael Ferreres
C. Antonio Sacramento
C. Ricardo Muñoz
Suay
Ciudad de
la Justicia
L'Oceanogràfic
Av. Hermanos
Maristas
Camino de las Moreras
Calle Antonio Ferrandis

0 ___ 1/4 mi
0 ___ 0.25 km

Arts & Entertainment A to Z

Casino
★ Gran Casino Monte Picayo
PUZOL   Offers 18 gaming tables, American and French roulette, Poker and Blackjack, and the usual slot machines. A 12.5mile/20km drive away with a five-star hotel attached. *Urb. Monte Picayo, Puzol.* ☎ *96-142-1211. www.cirsa.com/casinos/ monte_picayo. Daily 7pm–5am. Taxi or mainline train to Puzol and 20-min walk. Map p 115.*

Cinema
Cine Albatros UNIVERSIDAD
POLITÉCNICA   Multiscreen sister cinema to Ciné Babel (see below). *Pl. Fray Luis Colomer 4.* ☎ *96-393-2677. www.cinesalbatrosbabel.com. Bus: 30. Metro: Aragón, Universidad. Map p 116.*

Cine Babel ARAGÓN   Small and
intimate art-house multiplex cinema, showing mainly independent films from all around the world in VO (original version with Spanish subtitles). Both this and its sister cinema have a sandwich bar attached. *Sancho Tello 10.* ☎ *96-369-4530. www. cinesalbatrosbabel.com. Bus: 10, 12, 41, 79. Metro: Aragón. Map p 116.*

★ IVAC Filmoteca CENTRO
IVAC has regular cycles of films and events throughout the year. Each summer they run open-air cinemas in the Palau de la Música gardens and on the seafront at Malvarrosa— there's always a buzzing atmosphere and it's usually full. *Plaza Ayuntamiento 17.* ☎ *96-353-9299. www.ivac-lafilmoteca.es. Bus: 32, 70, 71,81. Metro: Xàtiva. Map p 115.*

★ UGC CINÉ CITÉ CAMPANAR
On the top floor of the Fuencarral (see p 66), this modern multiplex is the place to see mainstream films in VO (the original version). *Avda. Tirso de Molina 16.* ☎ *90-210-0842. www.ugc.es. Bus: 95. Metro: Túria. Map p 115.*

Classical Music & Opera
★★ Palau de la Música
ALAMEDA   A glass-and-marble building that's home to both the Orchestra of Valencia and to the Valencia Municipal Brass Band. The Palau has a first-rate reputation, and this is well deserved: you only have to look at the world-renowned international soloists, conductors, orchestras, and groups who visit, as well as the brilliant Jazz Festival, to see why. *Paseo de la Alameda 30.* ☎ *96-337-5020. www.palaude valencia.com. Bus: 2, 4, 10, 12, 95. Metro: Alameda. Map p 116.*

Palau de la Música.

★★★ Palau de les Arts Reina Sofia CIUDAD DE LAS ARTES Y LAS CIENCIAS

Architect Calatrava's innovative, state-of-the-art (both inside and out), opera house has a main auditorium, seating 2,500, and other smaller performance areas and auditoria. Tickets sell out almost as soon they go on sale. The season runs from October to June each year. *Autopista del Saler 1.* ☎ *96-316-3737 or 902-202-383. www.lesarts.com. Bus: 32, 95. Map p 116.*

Dance & Flamenco

★★ Café del Duende BOTANIC

Probably the most authentic, and certainly one of the best Flamenco performance bars in the city. It is tiny, and packed on Flamenco nights, particularly Thursdays and Fridays. *C/ Túria 62.* ☎ *63-045-5289. www. cafedelduende.com. Wed and Thurs 10pm–2.30am, Fri and Sat 10pm– 3.30am. Bus: 5b. Metro: Túria. Map p 115.*

★ La Buleria MONTE-OLIVET

Tablao Flamenco, which roughly translates as 'dinner and Flamenco', accurately describes what's on offer at La Buleria. This place is open at the weekends and provides a well-priced night of good food, authentic music, and dance. *C/ Obispo Jaime Pérez.* ☎ *96-315-3058/96-381-5661. www.labuleria.com. Thurs–Sun 9pm for the show at 11pm. Tapas and show 25€, dinner and show 45€. Bus: 35, 95. Map p 116.*

★ La Claca BARRIO DEL CARMEN

La Claca has been around since the late 1970s. Like Radio City, it is open every night but has a regular Sunday Flamenco show starting at around 11.30pm. *C/ San Vicente 3. No phone. www.laclaca.com. Tickets 5€–10€. Bus: 8, 9, 11, 70, 71. Map p 115.*

★ Radio City BARRIO DEL CARMEN

One of the best-known and loved multi-use venues in the city. The weekly program includes a Flamenco show every Tuesday evening at 11pm. Very busy. *C/ Santa Teresa 19.* ☎ *96-391-4151. www.radiocity valencia.com. Open daily early evening to 3.30am. Tickets 7€, includes a beer. Bus: 5b. Map p 115.*

Jazz

★ Black Note Club ARAGÓN

Jazz is definitely their 'thang' here. The free Black Note Jam Sessions on a Monday night are legendary. It is not unusual for a big international name in jazz to stop by and jam as they pass through the area on tour. *C/ Polo y Peyloron 15.* ☎ *96-393-3663. Mon–Sat 10pm–3.30/4.00am. Tickets between 5€ and 15€ depending on the act. Bus: 79, 80. Metro: Aragón. Map p 116. See p 110.*

★ Jimmy Glass Jazz Pub BARRIO DEL CARMEN

Smoky, dark, and cozy, this true jazz bar is a relaxing place to sit back and enjoy one of their 'large' drinks. Tuesdays are for old-style jazz, and there are live performances throughout the year. A few pool tables are at the back. *C/ Baja 28. www.jimmyglassjazz.net. No phone. Every night 9pm–1am. No cover. Bus: 5, 95. Map p 115.*

Sports

★★ Ágora CIUDAD DE LAS ARTES Y LAS CIENCIAS

Valencian-born Santiago Calatrava designed yet another spectacular building in La Ciudad de las Artes y las Ciencias for the Annual Spanish Open Tennis tournament, and (as of the time of writing) hopefully the Ágora will be completed just in time in October 2009. It will become Valencia's largest auditorium and will seat 5,000 people to be used for various cultural and sporting events. *Autopista del Saler.* ☎ *90-210-0031. Bus: 32, 95. Map p 116.*

Valencia Loves the Arts

Valencia has a wealth of theaters, cinemas, and performance spaces. However, at various times of the year performances take to the open air, with street and theater performances for free. Look out for The **Veo** international street performance (February), the **Eclectic**, a festival at CAC of performing arts including music and street theater (July), and the **Biennial**, an international art and performance festival (September to November 2009). There are also two annual film festivals whose reputations are growing internationally, *Mostra del Mediterraneo*, the Mediterranean Film Festival in October, and the festival of Young Filmmakers, *Cinema Jove* in June.

★★★ Circuito Ricardo Torno

CHESTE   Home to Moto GP racing since 1999, it plays host to all kinds of events including Touring Cars and Super Bikes. It is also a top venue for major music acts. *Autovia 25km/ 16 miles from Valencia on A3 Valencia–Madrid, exit 334.* ☎ *90-210-2899. www.circuitvalencia.com. During events there is a train service from Valencia. Map p 116.*

★★El Bosque

CHIVA   In a spectacular setting in the wooded hills above Godelleta, this 18-hole, 72-par golf course offers views towards Valencia and the sea. *Club de Golf El Bosque. A-3 direction Madrid, exit 337, Godelleta, km 4,1.* ☎ *96-180-8009. www.elbosquegolf.com.*

★★ El Escorpion

BÉTERA   A 27-hole, 72-par course with an old *masía* (mansion) as a clubhouse, superb facilities including pool and tennis courts, and a restaurant. *Club de Golf Escorpión. Ctra. S. Antonio Benagéber-Bétera, km 3. Bétera.* ☎ *96-160-1211. www.club escorpion.com. Metro: Bétera. Map p 116.*

★★★ El Saler

EL SALER   With a 72 par,18 holes and its attachment to the Parador Hotel in the Parque Naturaleza de L'Albufera, this is probably the closest golf club to Valencia. It's said to be one of the world's best, and was recently voted number two in Europe thanks to its wind conditions, which rival those of St. Andrews. *Club de Golf El Saler. Avda de los Pinares 151. (Parador de Turismo Luis Vives).* ☎ *93-161-9384. www.parador.es.*

★ Estadi Ciutat de València

BENIMACLET   This is the home of Valencia's other soccer team, Levante UD. The stadium is also occasionally used for concerts. *C/ San Vicente de Paul 44. www.levanteud. com. Bus: 11, 12, 16, 36, 70, 89, 90. Metro: Estadi del Llevant or Machado. Map p 115.*

★ Estadi Nou Mestalla

BENIMAMET   Valencia FC's (as in soccer) new home looks like an enormous shiny stress ball just waiting to be picked up and squished. It was the winning entry in a competition and, for once, I agreed with the judge's decision. Watch out on Saturdays for huge crowds near the stadium dressed in the team's color of orange. *Avda Cortes Valencianas. No phone. www.valenciacf.es. Bus: 62, 63. Metro: Beniferri. Map p 115.*

★★ Formula One European Grand Prix

MALVARROSA   2008

The new Estadi Nou Mestalla.

saw the first F1 Urban Circuit in Valencia. On a specially built track, the race took place around the Port of Valencia, now renamed Marina Juan Carlos I, and was a notable success. It is here for the next six years each August. *Marina Juan Carlos I.* ☎ *96-316-4007. www.valencia streetcircuit.com. Bus: 1, 2. Metro: Neptú. Tram: Dr Lluch. Map p 116.*

Port America's Cup PUERTO
When land-locked Switzerland won the America's Cup, it chose Valencia as the venue for the challenge in 2007. Valencia's dirty and decaying port was given new life and, for four years, it became home to the world's oldest sporting competition and teams of sailors from all over the world. When Switzerland won again in Valencia in 2007 they chose to stay here for the next competition. However, there have been legal wranglings in international courts ever since and the future of the America's Cup, as we go to press, is

still not certain. If it goes ahead there will be sailing regattas through 2009 and another America's Cup challenge in 2010. The city is crossing its fingers. *Marina Juan Carlos I. Bus: 1, 2. Metro: Neptú. Tram: Dr Lluch. Map p 116.*

★ **Trinquete Pelayo** CENTRO
This has to be the most curious of all sporting venues—quite possibly in the world—and is hidden away down a street close to Valencia Station. At the front it looks like any bar, but a door at the back leads to the court of the sport pilota (also known as pelota or even fronton). The 140-year-old court, nicknamed 'La Catedral', is to pilota what the UK's Wimbledon is to tennis. At around 60m/197ft long, it can hold a crowd of a thousand spectators. The game, a kind of handball, dates back to the 14th century and is still played all over Valencia, both in *trinquetes* (courts) and on village streets. The most important games are played

Watersports & Keeping Fit

There are many ways to take part in sport in the city or just beyond. On the beaches there are sailing and windsurfing schools. (Real Club Náutico Valencia C/ Canal, 91 ☎ 96-341-4110 and Club Náutico Port Saplaya, Ronda del Puerto s/n, Port Saplaya, Alboraya ☎ 96-355-0033. In the Río Túria park there are running tracks and football, basketball, and rugby pitches, with cycle/skate tracks all the way through.

Advance Tickets & Listings

For the latest concert, theater, and event listings, pick up a copy of the weekly *Túria,* a guide to all entertainment in Valencia. It's available at newsstands and is written in Spanish, but it's comprehensible even to non-Spanish speakers. An English guide *24/7 Magazine* publishes ten issues a year and is fairly good for listings; it is available in bars and the tourist offices.

Other helpful services are: **ServiEntrada** (☎ 902-11-55-77; www. bancaja.com); **ServiCam** (☎ 902-44-43-00; www.servicam.com); and **Tick Tack Ticket** (☎ 902-15-00-25; www.ticktackticket.com; from abroad ☎ 34/93-445-06-60).

here, and if you are in town on a Saturday you can watch the professionals. Oh, and by the way, the bar serves tasty tapas. *C/ Pelayo 6.* ☎ *96-352-6845. Bus: 5, 6, 7, 8, 19, 35, 40. Metro: Xàtiva. Map p 115.*

Theater

★ **Teatro Olympia** CENTRO Valencia's privately owned, Broadway-style theater regularly has the top touring Spanish musicals, comedies, and variety shows. *C/ San Vicente 44.* ☎ *96-392-1482. www. teatro-olympia.com. Bus: 8, 9, 11, 70, 71. Metro: Xàtiva. Map p 115.*

★ **Teatro Principal** CENTRO This is Valencia's oldest and largest theater; it has five tiers of balconies and boxes. Its program includes plays, opera, musical entertainment, and some of the biggest names in ballet. *C/ Barcas 15.* ☎ *96-353-9200. www. teatres.gva.es Closed August. Bus: 26, 31. Metro: Colón or Xàtiva. Map p 115.*

★ **Teatro Talia** BARRIO DEL CARMEN In the heart of the Carmen, another much smaller classic-style theater. It hosts lots of comedy, plays, and dance. *C/ Caballeros 31.* ☎ *96-391-2920. Bus: 5b. Map p 115.*

Celebrations at the America's Cup.

Las Fallas

★★★ **Las Fallas** ALL AROUND THE CITY AND BEYOND   March 15 each year sees the beginning of what has to be one of the most spectacular and exhilarating five days in all of Europe. Up to two million visitors come to watch or join, although they are mostly Spanish as Las Fallas seems to be a well-kept secret from the rest of the world. It is the most extraordinary festival, celebrated only in the Comunidad de Valencia and most of it in the city itself. The firework displays are incredible and can be seen both day and night—Máscletas are the daytime firework displays. The city is buzzing 24/7 and, if you have the stamina, you could party without a break. There are free concerts and dances throughout the city, and the bars and cafés stay open all hours to allow revelers to keep their strength up with food and drink. Look for the street markets and food vendors where you can buy a special type of doughnut called *Buñuelos*. Then there are the bullfights, exquisite costumes of the Falleras and Falleros, marching bands, and solemn processions. One procession, the Ofrenda, takes two days and consists of 150,000 Falleras and Falleros walking through the city. Mid-March is definitely one of the best times to visit Valencia.

Origins of the Festival

The festival is said to have pagan origins; carpenters would throw out old offcuts of wood into the street, setting fire to them to welcome spring. This tradition has grown into a huge festival. Up to 500 huge sculptures or Fallas are set up in almost every square on March 15. Each sculpture carries satirical four-line verses written in Valencian, and street parties take place by each one every day and night of the week. On the 19th, known as La Cremà, the Fallas are set alight and burned accompanied by fireworks and the whole city seems to be ablaze.

Las Fallas.

La Cremà—the burning of the Fallas.

Events

Planta–March 15 The night of the 15th is the 'planting' of the Fallas. All *casals* (organizing clubs), who have been working for a year to produce their individual pieces, need to have finished their Fallas by midnight for judging. Once all the Fallas are in place, they are judged by various categories such as sizes and poems. The top award-winners draw the biggest crowds.

La Ofrenda–March 17 & 18 *Ofrenda* is the giving of flowers to *La Virgen de los Desamparados* (The Virgin of the Deserted) in the Plaza de la Virgen (see p 10, bullet ⑫). On the 17th and 18th, a staggering 150,000 women and children, all dressed in the costume of Las Falleras, parade through the city from their respective casals along with marching brass bands and fellow members. They carry different-colored flowers, which match the flower robe created by that year's winning designer for the huge wooden figure of the Virgin. The procession converges on the Plaza de la Virgen and the flowers are handed over to be affixed to the Virgin—it is very moving to watch. The flowers are left in place for at least a week and are a wonderful sight.

San José–March 19 *San José* is Father's Day in Spain, and the busiest day of all the Fallas week.

La Cremà–March 19 *La Cremà* takes place on the night of the 19th and celebrates the burning of the Fallas. These beautifully crafted sculptures go out in a blaze of glory. The activity starts around 10pm, culminating at about 1am with the burning of the Fallas in the *Ayuntamiento* (Town Hall Square), accompanied by the very last firework display of the festival. Each burning is accompanied by its own individual firework extravaganza—you could be forgiven for thinking the city is on fire! Many *fallas* are 20 to 30m/ 65 to 100ft and can fall very close to the buildings. Firefighters from all over the region are bought in to the city to hose the surrounding buildings to protect them from damage while the fires blaze.

Costumes & People

Blusón If you want to be truly Valencian, buy yourself a *blusón* or overshirt. Said to originate from England in the 19th century, it is usually black or denim blue and is worn with a blue-and-white checked neck scarf.

Casal Las Fallas is organized by *casals*, social clubs that organize fundraising events and the design and building of the Fallas.

Fallera & Fallero A *Fallera* is a female of any age, who wears the traditional *fallera* outfit (often handed down through many generations). A new costume can cost 6,000€ or more. Each casal elects a queen, its *Fallera Mayor*, aged over 14, and the *Fallera Mayor Infantil* (under 14). A Fallera Mayor and Fallera Mayor Infantil of Valencia are selected from all the casals in the community. Those chosen consider it an enormous privilege, and even after Fallas they maintain a high profile, acting as ambassadors for Valencia and, on many occasions, even traveling abroad to promote the community. A *Fallero* is a man or boy who has chosen to dress in costume for Fallas.

Fallas & Ninots

Ninots A *ninot* is a single piece of the *Falla*, or sculpture. At least 30 to 50 ninots make up a Falla. Each one, usually intricately detailed, beautifully made and painted, is designed by an *àrtista*. A Falla can take a year to make by these specialist craftspeople in workshops and studios all over the community. The majority are made in *Ciudad Artista Fallero*, Fallas City, in Benicalap, an area devoted to the craft. The figures follow a topical, satirical, political, and usually comical theme. The average finished size of these works is 10 to 15m high, although some are much bigger.

Fireworks

Despertà Fireworks and marching bands wake up the city at around 7.30am for another day of Fiesta.

Mascletà Every day at precisely 2pm from March1 to 19, this daytime firework display, unique to Valencia, takes place. The noise is so loud that you are advised to keep your mouth open to avoid bursting your ear-drums! Its popularity means that it is not only shown live on television, but the sound is relayed live on the radio, too.

Petardos & Borrachos Loud bangers, it is as simple as that. You will not be able to escape them in the city.

Food & Drink

Buñuelos & Chocolate The Spanish love dunking, and *Chocolate con Churros* (hot chocolate with *Spanish donuts*) is a particular favorite. *Buñuelos* are a variation traditionally made just for Fallas. They are round and can be made plain or stuffed with pumpkin or figs—perfect for dunking in thick, hot chocolate. Stalls making and selling them can be found on virtually every street corner during Fallas. You'll pay around 6€ for a dozen (*docena*).

Horchata & Fartons *Horchata* (pronounced *or-chah'-tah*) is a delicious (non-alcoholic) sweet milky drink made from *chufas* (tiger nuts), small tubers grown in the fields around the city. Oh, and *fartons*? They are long sticky buns, served warm that you dunk in your *horchata*. Mmmmm!

Paella It's not unusual during Fallas to walk down a Valencian street and find it lined with the smells of cooking paellas along the road. These are either for competitions or cooking for a fiesta. If you are lucky, one of the revelers may offer you a taster!

Verbena A *verbena* is an outdoor party. During Fallas there are *verbenas* every night in the streets all over the city. The bars and music attract all ages and are jolly good, noisy fun. ●

Lodging Best Bets

Best **Designer Boutique Hotel**
★★★ Hospes Palau de la Mar $$$
C/ Navarro Reverter, 14 (p 131)

Best **Family Hotel**
★ Hotel Expo $$ Avda. Pio XII, 4.
(p 132)

Best **Value Hotel in the Center**
★ Hostal Venecia $ C/ En Llop, 5.
Plaza del Ayuntamiento (p 132)

Best **Escape to Golf**
★★ Ad Hoc Parque Hotel, Betera
$$$ C/ Sicilia 255 (p 130)

Best **Gay-friendly, Authentic
Valencian Neighborhood**
★★ ChillArt Hotel Jardin Botanico
$$ C/ Dr.Peset Cerera, 6 (p 131)

Best **Super Smart Hotel**
★★ Westin Valencia $$$$
C/ Amadeo de Saboya,16 (p 136)

Best **Beach Hotel**
★★★ Las Arenas Balneario $$$
C/ Eugenia Viñes, 22–24 (p 134)

Best **Cheap and Cheerful
Backpacker**
★ Purple Nest $$$ C/ La Paz, 36
(p 135)

Best **Designer Beach Boutique**
★ Hotel Neptuno $$$ Paseo de
Neptuno, 2 (p 133)

Best **Treat Out Of City**
★★ Mas De Canicatti $$$$ Villa-
marchante (p 134)

Best **Way-out Decor**
★★ Rooms Deluxe Hostel $$
Av. Instituto Obrero, 20 (p 136)

Best **Apartments**
★★ 40 flats $$ Av. Instituto Obrero,
20 (p 130)

Best **Location for Sightseeing**
★★ Hotel Apsis del Carmen $$$
C/ Blanquerias, 11 (p 132)

Most **Unusual Lobby**
★★ La Casa Azul $$ C/ Cardinal
Bulloch (p 134)

The Westin Valencia.

Beach Lodging

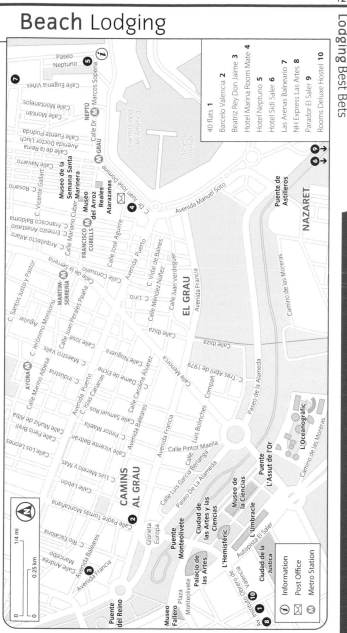

ⓘ Information

⊠ Post Office

Ⓜ Metro Station

Centro Histórico Lodging

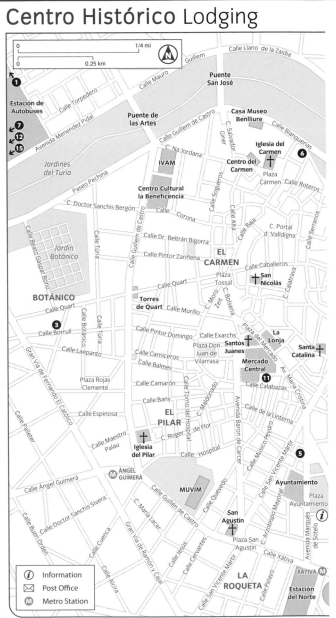

Ad Hoc Parque Hotel **1**
Astoria Palace **2**
ChillArt Hotel Jardin Botanico **3**
Hospes Palau de la Mar **4**
Hostal Venecia **5**
Hotel Apsis del Carmen **6**
Hotel Expo **7**
Hotel Petit Palace Bristol **8**
Hotel Vincci Lys **9**
Husa Reina Victoria **10**
La Casa Azul **11**
Mas De Canicattí **12**
Meliá Inglés Boutique Hotel **13**
Purple Nest **14**
Sercotel Sorolla Palace Hotel **15**
Westin Valencia **16**

Valencia Lodging A to Z

40 flats CIUDAD DE LAS ARTES Y LAS CIENCIAS   These modern purpose-built apartments are thoughtfully and carefully kitted out with everything you might need. Each smart, designer flat sleeps up to six people so they're ideal for larger families. Located just 100m/300ft from La Ciudad de las Artes y las Ciencias and close to the city center, they are in the same building as Rooms Deluxe (see p 136) and share the same reception area and friendly staff. *Av. Instituto Obrero, 20.* ☎ *96-335-6793. www.40flats. com. www.likeathome.net. 101 rooms. Doubles 85€–145€. AE, DC, MC, V. Bus: 35, 95. Map p 127.*

★ Ad Hoc Parque Hotel BÉTERA Located 20 minutes out of the city, this hotel sits opposite El Scorpion (see p 119), golf club and is close to good riding stables. The bedrooms are light and attractive; all have balconies and old-style wooden shutters. Its pretty restaurant, La Sal, has an interesting menu of fresh Mediterranean gourmet cuisine and a very good reputation locally. *Urbanización Torre en Conill. Bétera.* ☎ *96-169-8393. www. adhochoteles.com. 40 rooms. Doubles 100€–200€. AE, DC, MC, V. Car or taxi. Map p 128.*

★★ Astoria Palace CENTRO Offering a more traditional (and slightly faded) style, this is one of the oldest hotels in Valencia and is very centrally located in a quiet corner of a delightful plaza just off the main square. The rooms are large, comfortable, and traditional. On the roof, you can enjoy the indoor leisure center and gym, Jacuzzi, and sauna with views of the city center. *Plaza de Rodrigo Botet, 5.* ☎ *96-398-1000. www.hotelastoria palace.com. 169 rooms. Doubles 125€–200€, w/breakfast. AE, DC, MC, V. Bus: 4, 6, 10, 13, 16, 36, 62, 72, 81. Metro: Xàtiva Map p 128.*

★ Barcelo Valencia CIUDAD DE LAS ARTES Y LAS CIENCIAS   Outside, it has a black glass box appearance, inside an airy, modern interior with bright-colored glass panels and attractive artwork. If you ask for one

Modern, conveniently situated apartments at 40 flats.

Astoria Palace, situated in a quiet plaza.

of the rooms at the front, you are guaranteed views of La Ciudad de las Artes y las Ciencias. The rooms are ultra modern and just a little soulless for my taste, although I loved the glass walk-in shower. The restaurant has amusing theme weeks at intervals throughout the year and the rooftop spa offers many therapies and treatments. *Av. de Francia, 11 (esq. Padre Toms Montaa).* ☎ *96-330-6344. www. barcelovalencia.com. 187 rooms. Doubles 175€–300€, w/breakfast. AE, DC, MC, V. Bus: 35, 95. Map p 127.*

★★★ Beatriz Rey Don Jaime
ALAMEDA With 14 floors, this stately hotel offers city views from most of the rooms. Ideally situated opposite the Palau de la Música if you fancy popping along for a concert, it is only a 10-minute walk into the city center. The rooms are large and decorated in muted tones. Head up to the rooftop pool from May to October for views across the Túria. The hotel runs a free bus service to the beach for its clients throughout the day. *Avenida de Baleares, 2.* ☎ *96-337-5030. www.beatrizhoteles. com. 318 rooms. Doubles 95€–180€.*

AE, DC, MC, V. Metro: Jaume I or Drassanes. Map p 127.

★ ChillArt Hotel Jardin Botanico BOTANICO This charming, comfortable, arty hotel with its funky decor and original artwork consistently gets the thumbs-up from guests who love the friendly, helpful staff. It has 16 impeccably decorated rooms, each with a Jacuzzi bathroom. A gay-friendly hotel. *C/ Dr. Peset Cerera 6.* ☎ *96-315-4012. www.hotel jardinbotanico.com. 16 rooms. Doubles 70€–120€, w/breakfast. AE, DC, MC, V. Metro: Túria. Map p 128.*

★★ Hospes Palau de la Mar
RAVAL A magnificent, heritage-listed, 19th-century stately home in the heart of the city. You enter through the classical exterior to an exceptionally white, bright, modern, and elegant interior: minimalist design with a sleek courtyard garden. The guest rooms are masterpieces, all smooth surfaces, and straight lines. The cool cocktail bar looks out onto the courtyard and Senzone, the restaurant, has an interesting Mediterranean menu. The Wellness Center occupies two light-filled floors. It is all so

Hospes Palau de la Mar.

perfect you feel you should talk in whispers. *C/ Navarro Reverter, 14.* ☎ *96-316-2884. www.hospes.es. 66 rooms. Doubles 175€–600€. AE, DC, MC, V. Bus: 5b, 6, 9, 11, 16, 31, 32, 36, 70, 95. Metro: Colón or Alameda. Map p 128.*

★ **Hostal Venecia** CENTRO A great find this one; my wife and I book this place for our friends when we are full up at home. It is categorized as a hostel, but only because it doesn't have a formal reception area. Bedrooms are comfortable with full en-suite bathrooms and probably some of the best views of the Plaza del Ayuntamiento. Brilliantly priced, considering its location, it offers family rooms and smoking rooms, too. *Calle En Lop 5.* ☎ *90-099-0011 or 96-352-4267. www.hotelvenecia.com. 54 rooms. Doubles 55€–120€. AE, DC, MC, V. Bus: 8, 9, 11, 70, 71. Metro: Xàtiva. Map p 128.*

★ **Hotel Apsis del Carmen** BARRIO DEL CARMEN Smart modern and very Carmen. This hotel offers a highly personal service. The bedrooms have wooden floors, marble bathrooms and are decorated in shades of cream and brown. There's

also a rooftop terrace with a Jacuzzi. A wonderful location for sightseeing, it is just a walk away from all the major sights. *C/ Blanquerías, 11.* ☎ *93-272-4140. www.hotel-del carmenvalencia.com. 25 rooms. Doubles 90€–120€, w/breakfast. AE, DC, MC, V. Bus: 5, 5b, 95. Map p 128.*

★ **kids Hotel Expo** NUEVO CENTRO This busy great-value hotel is just over the river by Nuevo Centro, a short bus or metro ride into the city. A large rooftop pool and terrace bar is a welcome feature if you are holidaying here in the summer. The rooms are adequately equipped and the staff is friendly and helpful. The piano bar is a good meeting point. *Avda. Pio XII, 4.* ☎ *96-303-3600. www.expohotelvalencia.com. 378 rooms. Doubles 52€–95€. AE, DC, MC, V. Bus: 1, 8, 62, 63, 79, 95. Metro: Túria. Map p 128.*

★★ **Hotel Marina Room Mate** MALVARROSA The rooms are a little stark but well equipped and the upper rooms have views of the Formula One track to the front so if you are a fan, ask for one of these. There is a small rooftop Jacuzzi and gym, and a modern, elegant bar and restaurant. *Plaza Tribunal de las*

Aguas, 4. ☎ 96-320-3010. www.
room-matehotels.com. 42 rooms.
Doubles 70€–110€, w/breakfast. AE,
DC, MC, V. Bus: 1, 2, 20, 21, 23. Metro:
Neptú. Map p 127.

★ **Hotel Neptuno** MALVARROSA
Clean, simple, and stylish, and in a
privileged position on the beach at
Malvarrosa. All the bright, spacious
guest rooms have views to the beach
or to the Marina Juan Carlos I. There
is a delightful restaurant overlooking
the beach and a rooftop sun terrace
with a tiny dip pool to cool you down
on hot days. *Paseo de Neptuno 2.*
☎ 96-356-7777. www.hotelneptuno
valencia.com. 48 rooms. Doubles
180€–225€. AE, DC, MC, V. Metro:
Neptú. Map p 127.

★★★ **Hotel Petit Palace Bristol** CENTRO   A fantastic location in
a quiet street right in the center of
the city makes this boutique hotel,
set in a beautiful 19th-century
palace, a chic place to stay. The
high-tech rooms have exercise bikes,
flat screen computers, and hydro-
massage showers, and the family
rooms have twin or king size beds
and bunks. The hotel offers free
bike hire for its guests. *C/ L'Abadia
de San Martin 3.* ☎ 96-394-5100.

www.hotelpetitpalacebristol.com. 43
rooms. Doubles 95€–140€. AE, DC,
MC, V. Bus: 31, 36, 70, 71. Metro:
Colón. Map p 128.

Hotel Sidi Saler EL SALER   With
its idyllic position and wonderful
views across the dunes to the sea,
this hotel should be the perfect
place to stay, but because it needs a
bit of a facelift it's not as good as it
could be. Only 20 minutes from the
city, it has its own regular bus service into Valencia and features a
large pool, gardens, a gym, bars, a
restaurant, and sports of all kinds.
Playa El Saler ☎ 96-161-0411. www.
sidisaler.com. 276 rooms. Doubles
135€–200€. AE, DC, MC, V. Metrobus,
car, or taxi. Map p 127.

Hotel Vincci Lys CENTRO   A
modern and à la mode hotel, the
guest rooms have all the amenities
you need and are decorated in warm
colors. Another good, centrally
located hotel, between Calle Colón,
the main shopping street, and the
Ayuntamiento (Town Hall Square), it
is the only hotel in the city center
with its own parking. *C/ Martinez
Cubells, 5.* ☎ 96-350-9550 or 901-
988-504. www.hotelvinccilys.com.
101 rooms. Doubles 160€–200€.

The Borgia room at La Casa Azul.

An attractive view from a bedroom at Melià Inglés Boutique Hotel.

AE, DC, MC, V. Bus: 5, 5b, 13, 62, 81. Metro: Xàtiva Map p 128.

★★ **Husa Reina Victoria** CENTRO Originally built in 1913 but recently renovated, this is a pleasing Art Nouveau hotel. Rooms are large and comfortable. It's right in the center and good value considering its location. *C/ Barcas 4–6.* ☎ *96-352-0487. www. husareinavictoria.com. 97 rooms. Doubles 90€–150€. AE, DC, MC, V. Bus: 5, 13, 32, 62, 81. Metro: Colón. Map p 128.*

La Casa Azul CENTRO   A wine shop on the ground floor acts as reception for the city's smallest hotel. La Casa Azul is a bright blue building and has only three rooms—one per floor, each of which is outrageously designed and decorated using a different theme. My favorite, the Borgia room, is full of fine antiques, including a piano. A highly decorative carved four-poster bed and other exquisite Oriental antiques furnish The Silk Route room. The Moon of Valencia room is all blue and contemporary cool. At the top is a gorgeous roof terrace. *C/ Cardinal Bulloch.* ☎ *96-351-1100. www.lacasaazul vinosandrooms.com. 3 rooms. Doubles 100€–125€. AE, DC, MC, V. Bus: 81. Metro: Xàtiva. Map p 128.*

★★ **kids** **Las Arenas Balneario** MALVARROSA   This grand hotel by the sea is an impressive sight on arrival. The reception looks right onto splendid terraces, gardens and fountains, the pool and, across the promende, the sea. Set at either end of the garden are two striking Parthenon-style buildings, home to banqueting and conference rooms. Most of the large guest rooms have balconies overlooking the gardens and views to the sea. All the luxury and finesse one would expect from a five-star luxury hotel. *C/ Eugenia Viñes, 22–24.* ☎ *96-312-0600. www. hotel-lasarenas.com. 253 rooms. Doubles (2-BR apt) 195€–800€. AE, DC, MC, V. Bus: 20, 22, 23. Metro: Neptú. Tram Dr Lluch. Map p 127.*

★ **kids** **Mas De Canicattí** VILLAMARCHANTE   Half an hour out of Valencia and up a sumptuous green driveway, this exquisite hideaway country hotel has every luxury, including a splendid spa and the first-class El Cadec restaurant. The guest rooms are spacious and elegant; there is even a suite with its own terrace and private pool. Check their website for specialty breaks, from wine tasting to spa weekends. *Ctra Pedralba 2, 9km.* ☎ *96-165-0534.*

www.masdecanicatti.com. 27 rooms. Doubles 250€–600€. AE, DC, MC, V. By car or taxi. Map p 128.

Melià Inglés Boutique Hotel

CENTRO   This converted neo-classical 18th-century palace is next door to the palacio that houses the National Ceramics Museum, and is on the city's most exclusive shopping street. Their coffee shop is a favorite with well-dressed shoppers. The rooms are large with high ceilings and are, as you would expect in a boutique hotel, plush and well appointed. A handy location for sightseeing on foot; most of the major sights are an easy walk away. *Marqués de dos Aguas, 6.* ☎ *96-351-6426. www.hotelinglesboutique. com. 63 rooms. Doubles 120€–150€. AE, DC, MC, V. Bus: 9, 11, 30, 31, 70, 71. Metro: Xàtiva. Map p 128.*

★ kids NH Express Las Artes

CIUDAD DE LAS ARTES Y LAS CIENCIAS   Smart and modern, perfect for business and pleasure. In a superb location, right by the La Ciudad de las Artes y las Ciencias, it also has easy access to the motorways out of the city. The rooms are comfortable and well equipped—with a choice of pillows. *Instituto*

Obrero de Valencia, 26–28. ☎ *96-335-6062. www.nh-hotels.com. 41 rooms. Doubles 62€–120€. AE, DC, MC, V. Bus: 35, 95. Map p 127.*

★ Parador El Saler EL SALER

The Parador El Saler nestles in sand dunes on the beach, many of the bedrooms enjoying breathtaking views to the sea. Excellent facilities include a spa, a gym, a pool (in season), and what is thought to be one of the world's best golf courses (see p 119), designed by specialist Spanish golf architect Javier Arana. The hotel and golf course are in the middle of the splendid green Natural Park of the Albufera. *Avda de los Pinares, 151.* ☎ *96-161-1186. www. parador.es. 19 rooms. Doubles 220€–350€, w/breakfast. AE, DC, MC, V. Car or taxi. Map p 127.*

★★ Purple Nest L'EIXAMPLE

Nest is a small group of hostels, offering the 'new backpacker' style of accommodation. Gone are the days of seedy, dreary dorms and nothing else, these hostels offer everything from your own room to sharing with up to 12 in an attractive clean and air-conditioned dormitory. Very reasonable rates, superb kitchens, lounges, Internet

Quirky decor at the Rooms Deluxe Hostel.

The Westin Valencia's terrace.

access, and even chillout roof top terraces. Check their website for Nest locations in Valencia. *C/ La Paz 36.* ☎ *96-342-7168. www.nesthostels valencia.com. 66 rooms. Doubles and dormitories from 14€. AE, DC, MC, V. Bus: 31, 36, 70, 71. Metro: Colón. Map p 128.*

★★ Rooms Deluxe Hostel
LA CIUDAD DE LAS ARTES Y LAS CIENCIAS   A unique idea in hostelling, this first-class hostel has a choice of 28 zanily themed bedrooms. Designed by 28 different artists, they are pure fantasy and all have smart en-suite bathrooms. You can choose to sleep in a swimming pool, a Buddhist temple, space odyssey, or one of 25 more styles. In the communal areas, there is a well-equipped kitchen and comfortable lounge to share with your fellow travelers, and free breakfast is on offer each day. A real treat for back-packers, but nobody said it has to be just for them. *Av. Instituto Obrero, 20.* ☎ *96-381-5339. www.roomsdeluxe.com. 28 rooms. Doubles 70€–100€, w/breakfast. AE, DC, MC, V. Bus: 35, 95. Map p 127.*

★★ Sercotel Sorolla Palace
Hotel BENIFERI   An ultra-modern and attractive luxury hotel right next door to the Palau de Congresos and therefore an ideal location for conference visitors. The guest rooms are attractively furnished and decorated in muted shades, with free wi-fi. The Sorolla Palace has the added bonus of a covered rooftop swimming pool, so whenever you visit you will be able to swim. *Avda. de las Cortes Valencianas, 58.* ☎ *96-186-8700. www.hotelsorollapalace.com. 154 rooms. Doubles 175€–600€, w/breakfast. AE, DC, MC, V. Bus: 62. Metro: Beniferri. Map p 128.*

★ Westin Valencia ALAMEDA
One of the newest five-star plus hotels in Valencia. Elegant and set around a large internal garden it feels more like a country hotel. There is a superb choice of bars and restaurants, and an excellent spa. Each room has the luxurious trademark Westin Heavenly bed and showers. If you feel indulgent, treat yourself and book into the suite. Designed by top Valencian dress designer Montesino (see p 59), it is an over-the-top, two-roomed suite with a private Jacuzzi under the stars. *C/ Amadeo de Saboya, 16.* ☎ *96-362-5900. www. westin.com/valencia. 135 rooms. Doubles 175€–890€. AE, DC, MC, V. Bus: 9, 29, 31, 70, 71, 81. Metro: Alameda. Map p 128.* ●

Benidorm

1. Playa del Levante
2. La Cava Aragonesa
3. Parc de l'Aigüera
4. Restaurante Marisquería Club Naútico
5. Altea
6. El Negro de Altea
7. Palau Altea

Horizonte

Altea

El Verdader

Urbanització la Foia Blanca

l'Alfas del Pi

Jardin de Alfaz

l'Albir

Mar Mediterráneo

Urbanització Panorama

les Coves

Autopista del Mediterraneo

Avenida de la Comunidad Valenciana

Benidorm

Avenida de Europa

(A7) Road Number

0 —— 1 mi
0 —— 1 km

Benidorm is a two-hour drive from Valencia and a world away in culture. However, it is worth a visit to this 'Manhattan' by the sea, if only to compare it to Valencia. Like it or loathe it, you can't fail to be amused and amazed by it. My wife and I feel like we are 'abroad' when we make our one or two annual trips there. Why do we go? Because it is fun and interesting to see a city that keeps reinventing itself. START: **Autopista A7 (direction Alicante), south 139km/86miles to Benidorm.**

---

1 ★★ kids Playa del Levante. The skyline as you approach Benidorm on the Autopista A7 is a real surprise: the high-rise buildings are so tall you could be forgiven for thinking you were looking at the Manhattan skyline. Benidorm sits in a large bay and the 1.4mile/3km long, 80m wide beach, Playa del Levante fronts the towering part of this city of fun. A spotlessly clean blue flag beach heaves with toasting

bodies not only in the summer, but also at almost any time of the year. The promenade is lined with bars offering happy hours and live entertainment; smart restaurants jostle for space with bars and shops. In the few blocks back from the beach, English, German, and Dutch bars and pubs tout impossibly cheap breakfasts and meals on offer everywhere. Constant processions of people wander up and down its

More Than Meets the Eye...

Ever since its explosion as a major tourist resort in the 1960s, Benidorm has constantly reinvented itself, especially thanks to its visionary former mayor, Pedro Zaragoza, who died in 2008. A staggering five million people visit each year—of whom more than half are Spanish—and the city has 60,000 hotel beds, which have an average annual occupancy of 90 percent. Its resident population is 74,000. There are said to be more fiestas celebrated in Benidorm than anywhere else in Spain—well over 50 each year. They are not staged, as cynics might assume, specifically for the tourist; the city is simply populated with people from all over Spain, and each group has brought with it its own traditions. Benidorm celebrates them all: from the outrageously costumed Moros y Cristianos festival to Fallas and the city's own five-day Fiesta in November celebrating its Patron Saints.

length and everywhere there are flyers for restaurants, tea dances, clubs, and bars. Benidorm in winter is the playground of Spanish *jubilados* (a happy-sounding word meaning 'pensioners') from the colder parts of northern Spain. It is always amusing to see them wrapped up in coats and scarves as they pass foreign tourists in shorts and t-shirts. At the end of Playa Levante, the Balcon del Mediterraneo, a large rock that was once a fortress protecting the inhabitants from pirates, is now a viewing point that separates Playa Levante from Playa Poniente. ⏰ *Half a day or more.* *100 km south of Valencia, on the Autopista A7. Benidorm Tourist Office, Avda de l'Aigüera s/n.* ☎ *96-585-5500 (Ayuntamiento de Benidorm).*

Benidorm's beach, Playa del Levante.

2 La Cava Aragonesa. More than 41m/134ft of selected tapas and canapés as well as 20 different plates of cold meats and cheeses greet you as you walk into this bar, and they are all labeled in Spanish and English. They have a proper restaurant too, which offers a well-priced menu del día at 12€. As you would expect by its name, it has an extensive selection of wines. *Daily 12–3.30pm and 6pm onwards. Plaza de la Constitución.* 96-680-1206. www.lacavaaragonesa.es. $$.

3 ★ Parc de l'Aigüera. This Neoclassical park is an interesting place to take a walk, or to sit with a book. Entering the park, you pass under a large, modern glass building, the *Ayuntamiento* (town hall), its pale green glass etched with over 60,000 names of its citizens from the last census before its completion. Throughout the month of August the amphitheater at the vast new Parc de l'Aigüera, near the old town hosts free concerts most nights. At the top end of the park is the Plaza de Toros, which, at various times of the year, has not only bullfights, but also concerts from internationally famous names. 🕓 *1 hr. Avda de l'Aigüera s/n.* 96-585-5500 (Ayuntamiento de Benidorm).

4 Restaurante Marisquería Club Naútico. People from all walks of life come here: well-coiffed ladies-who-lunch and be-suited businessmen eat and drink beside workmen and tourists. As with most bars in Spain they serve the best coffee, infusions (teas), hot chocolate, as well as cooling and thirst-quenching drinks, beers, and cocktails. *Paseo de Colón s/n.* 96-585-5425. $$.

5 ★★ **kids** Altea. On the drive back to Valencia, take a little detour into this very attractive town. It could not be more of a contrast to its near neighbor. It has a narrow, pebbly beach and a seafront road lined on one side with shops, bars, and restaurants. In fact, everything you'd expect of a smaller seaside resort including a small fishing harbor. Altea was 'discovered' in the 1960s by a hippie crowd and there is still an 'arty' feel to the place, nowhere more so than in the *casco antiguo* (historic center) that crowns the hill, with gorgeous views across the bay. This picture-book white Spanish village has a striking blue-domed church, **5A** Iglesia Virgen del Consuelo, in the cobbled main square, and this part of town is filled with galleries, shops, bars, and restaurants and, during high summer, there is a delightful nighttime street market selling handicrafts. The *casco antiguo* buzzes at night with lively bar and restaurant terraces full of locals and visitors alike, chatting, eating, and drinking. Each year the local **Facultat de Bellas Artes** (School of Fine Art) organizes an exhibition of

Practical Matters: Benidorm

There are no trains to Benidorm from Valencia; better to hire a car or take the daily luxury coach services from Valencia Coach Station which are bookable online at www.alsa.es and take about two hours each way, costing around 30€.

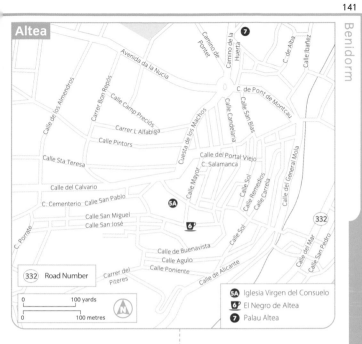

Altea

Avenida da la Nucia

Camino de Pontet

Camino de la Huerta

Calle Ibañez

C. de Alba

C. de Pont de Montcau

Calle San Blas

Calle Candelaria

Calle de los Almendros

Carrer Bon Repós

Calle Camp Precios

Carrer L Alfabiga

Calle Pintors

Cuesta de los Machos

Calle del Portal Viejo

Calle del General Mola

Calle Sta Teresa

C. Salamanca

Calle Mayor

Calle Sol

Calle del Calvario

C. Cementerio Calle San Pablo

Calle Remedios

Calle Cartela

Calle San Miguel

5A

Calle San José

6

Calle Sol

332

C. Porrate

Calle de Buenavista

Calle del Mar

Calle San Pedro

332 Road Number

Carrer del Piteres

Calle Agulo

Calle Poniente

Calle de Alicante

| 0 | 100 yards |
| 0 | 100 metres |

5A Iglesia Virgen del Consuelo
6 El Negro de Altea
7 Palau Altea

paintings, which decorate the balconies of the buildings in the narrow streets and squares in this part of town. ⏱ *2 hr. A7 (direction Valencia) 11 km/7miles from Benidorm.*

6 El Negro de Altea. Not quite in the casco antiguo, this restaurant is famous for its meat and for its spectacular views across the bay. What better way to watch the sunset than with a sundowner drink here, though if you can fit another meal in, they serve an excellent *pierna de cordero*, a small and succulent roast leg of lamb for one, delicious! *C/ Santa Barbara 4, Altea 03590.* ☎ *96-584-1826. $$.*

7 ★★ Palau Altea. Not far from the old town, Palau Altea is an excellent arts center. This new building is quite lovely and has a wonderful, large cupola ceiling in the main auditorium. The Palau has a varied and imaginative timetable of events, concerts, and exhibitions throughout the year. ⏱ *20 min. C/ Alcoy 18, 03590 Altea.* ☎ *96-688-1924. www. palaualtea.com. Opening hours vary.*

Altea beach side.

Requena & Utiel

A3   Road Number

Utiel
7 6 5
← 4

(A3)
(E901)

San
Antonio

Autopista del Este

3
2 1
Requena

(322)

1 Iglesia de Santa Maria
2 Cuevas de la Villa
3 Meson del Vino
4 Bodega Torre Oria
5 Museo del Vino
6 Cooperativa Agricola Utiel
7 Peña Taurina Utielana

0   3 mi
0   3 km

Just under an hour's drive from Valencia are flatlands more than 45km in diameter, the largest and highest (1,000m) in the Comunidad. The climate here is extreme: baking hot in summer and freezing cold in winter. It is, however, the ideal climate for wine making, and the towns of Utiel and Requena are now the largest wine producers in the province, and also the second largest producers of red wine in the country. START: **By car, take the A-111 towards Madrid; it's about an hour's drive.**

1 ★★ Iglesia de Santa Maria. At Requena's center is La Villa, the attractive and slightly ramshackle Medieval *casco historico* (historic center). Originally an 8th-century Moorish medina, it is certainly worth exploring; there are more than a few architectural treasures to be found within its tangled streets. Particularly beautiful is the intricate and ornate Gothic door to the Baroque decorated Iglesia de Santa Maria. This church was originally built in the 14th century but was embellished in the 18th. A fine church but fortunately they left the saints and Gothic motifs of this magnificent door untouched. Legend has it that the Knight El Cid lived here for a while in the Palacio del Cid prior to the reconquest. ⏰ *1hr. Plaza El Salvador s/n.* ☎ *96-230-0186. Daily all day. Admission free.*

Fine Wine, Fine Food

Both Requena and Utiel feature on the Denominación de Origen Utiel-Requena (a regulatory classification system for Spanish wines similar to the French appellations), but the former is the more attractive and is a lively and prosperous town. Originally famous in the 18th century for its fantastic silk textiles, the plain was once abundant with mulberry trees. Now it is grapevines that give the region its place in history, and it is famed for both its red and white wines—the award-winning cavas are said (quietly) to rival French champagnes. This is also game and *embutido* (sausage) country. The traditional Requena sausage is considered the sausage equivalent of wine's Denominación de Origen. Requena has excellent food shops too, selling hams and locally produced sausage, from the delicious *morcilla de cebolla* (black pudding made with onion) to spicy chorizos. **Carniceria Emilia** (C/ Fortaleza 10, Requena ☎ 96-230-3410) is one of my favorites.

② **Cuevas de la Villa.** What visitors find particularly fascinating about this old town is the Cuevas de la Villa. These man-made caves, virtually two towns, one above the other, were once used as homes and warehouses. Some of the caves can be viewed but they are mainly used for storage, sometimes with enormous (up to 3m tall) earthenware jars used for storing olive oil and wine. The entrance is in Plaza de Albornoz. ⏱ *1hr. La Villa Requena, Oficina de Turismo de Requena.* ☎ *96 2303851. www.requena.es. Adults 3€, children 2€. Tues-Sun 11am-1pm & Fri-Sun 5-7pm.*

③ **Meson del Vino.** One of Requena's oldest restaurants and certainly the best known and loved, you need to bring a healthy appetite. High-calorie stews, like their delicious, prize-winning Gazpacho Manchego, made with rabbit, partridge, and torn bits of flat bread, are a typical menu item and should keep you going for the rest of the day. The town's famous *embutidos (sausages)* are a specialty. As you walk into this bustling bar and restaurant, the huge head of a bull hanging on the wall greets you. *Avenida Arrabal.* ☎ *96-230-0001. $$$.*

Storage pots in Requena Caves.

The Best Day Trips & Excursions

④ Bodega Torre Oria. Any journey to the area must include at least one visit to a *bodega* or winery to sample some of the fine wines and cavas that are lovingly bottled here. There are more than 100 wineries in the area, producing from a few thousand bottles a year to millions. Most offer guided tours and wine tastings. Bodega Torre Oria, named for its onion-domed tower, is just outside the town on the road to Utiel. The buildings of this bodega are wonderful examples of *Modernista* architecture. Their cellars cover a staggering 5,000 sq m/53,800 sq ft, with more than six million bottles maturing, including a million bottles of cava. The bodega offers 45-minute tours, bookable by phone, which include tastings. ⏱ *45 min. Ctra Pontón-Utiel km 3, 03590 Altea.* ☎ *96-232-0289. www.torreoria.com. Jan–Oct Mon–Fri 8am–4.30pm, Sat 10am–2pm; Nov–Dec Sat 10am–2pm and 4pm–6pm, Sun 10am–2pm. Admission free.*

⑤ ★ Museo del Vino, Utiel. Lacking Requena's appealing prettiness, Utiel still has a lot to offer. Its very good museum of wine, aptly

Elaborate doorway, Requena.

named Museo del Vino, which is housed in a circular bodega, shows how wine is made. There is also winemaking equipment from down the ages on display here. The museum is home to the headquarters of the Asociación Ruta del Vino de la Denominación de Origen Utiel-Requena, (☎ 96-230-3772, www.rutavino.com), which naturally, with such superb wine country, offers *rutas* (wine tours). Working with

Practical Matters: Utiel & Requena

- **Requena Tourist Information Office:** C/ García Montés s/n, beside the entrance to La Vila (☎ 96-230-3851; www.requena.es).
- **Trains** (1 hr 20 minutes; ☎ 902-24-02-02; www.renfe.es) run around four times a day from Valencia Station, Estación del Norte.
- **Lodging** in Requena: **Casa Doña Anita**, Plaza Albornóz, 15 (☎ 96-230-5347; www.tubal.net; doubles 43€–57€). Small, antique-filled, and beautifully restored home on the edge of the historic La Villa.
- **Lodging** in Utiel: **Hotel Rural Entreviñas (Finca EL Renegado)**, 46315 Caudete de las Fuentes (☎ 96-123-5076; doubles 56€–85€ w/breakfast, apartments 115€–152€ including breakfast). Lovely old farmhouse with oak-beamed rooms, set in a vineyard and bodega.

Fairs & Festivals

Requena celebrates the pig and the sausage each year in February with **Muestra del Embutido de Artesano** (the sausage fair). For three days, wineries and food manufacturers of the area get together to offer samples of their wares to the public. A few euros buy you a wine glass, a small earthenware dish, and a sheet of tickets—wander around the stalls of your choice and exchange tickets for a fill of your glass or dish. In late August each year Requena celebrates the harvest with the **Fiesta de la Vendima**—you should be prepared for lots of throwing of water and some serious wine drinking. Utiel has the fiesta **Utiel Gastronomica** at the end of October, (neighboring Requena has an **Embutido** festival in February), with a tapas trail around the town.

other businesses in the area, this association offers one-day or weekend tours to bodegas and growers. The *rutas* include meals, sampling the local produce, and overnight accommodation if the tour falls on a weekend. The *rutas* are great value at 30€ for the day trip or from 95–170€ depending on the kind of accommodation for the weekend. The weekend offer includes visits to three bodegas, two heritage centers, two lunches, dinner, and a bed for the night. ⏱ *2 hr. Calle Sevilla 12, Utiel.* ☎ *96-217-1062. Admission free. Mon–Fri 10am–2pm.*

❻ Cooperativa Agricola Utiel. If you are after well-priced wines then the Cooperativa Agricola Utiel is the place for you. Here you can see the huge vats where the wine is produced and you can buy the end product in the *Despacho de Vinos.* ⏱ *30 min. Avda Martin Lázaro 8, Utiel.* ☎ *96-217-1468. Admission free. Mon–Fri (except Thurs) 9am–2pm & 4–7pm, Sat and Sun 9am–noon.*

❼ Peña Taurina Utielana (Plaza de Toros). The people of Utiel are extremely proud of their

bullring: it is the second largest after Valencia's and, built in 1858, is one of the oldest in the Comunidad. ⏱ *20 min. C/ Dos de Mayo s/n.* ☎ *96-217-1857. Bullfights: Mar, Jun, Sept. Museum Avda Marin Lázaro Tues–Sat 9am–2pm.* ☎ *96-217-3276.*

Utiel.

Peñiscola & Morella

0   5 mi
0   5 km

(A7) Road Number

Rossell

Vallibona

Morella

(232)

Canet lo Roig

Vallivana

Traiguera

San Jorge

Chert

Anroig

La Jana

(232)

Cati

Sant Mateu

Cálig

Tirig

La Salzadella

(340)

Mas d'En Rieres

Santa Magdalena de Pulpis

Peñiscola

(A7)

(E15)

1 Peñiscola
2 Mandarina Restaurant, Terraza, Café
3 Morella
4 Hotel Cardenal Ram

The two resorts of Peñiscola and Morella are at the northern end of the Comunidad Valenciana. Peñiscola, or Ciudad en la Mar, the 'city in the sea', is so named because it is very nearly an island, joined to the mainland only by a narrow strip. Its castle at the top of the outcrop became famous as the location for the film *El Cid*. The fortified town of Morella, clinging to a hilltop high above the area known as Els Ports, is said to be one of the oldest in Spain.
START: **Peñiscola is 93 miles/150km north of Valencia by car on the Carretera A7 (direction Castellon/Barcelona).**

1 ★ **Peñiscola.** Peñiscola is a small resort with a long promenade and sandy beach. It is sheltered at one end by an outcrop, covered by fortified, walls and an old town that is a picturebook white Spanish village. A maze of tiny cobbled streets are filled with ceramics and souvenir shops, and small houses lead the way up to the highest part, which boasts a 13th-century castle. The

city was fortified at this time and St Peter's Gate was used as a landing stage by the 14th-century AntiPope Benedict XIII, or Papa Luna. His coat of arms is still to be seen at its center. The castle is well worth the climb through the narrow streets; not only are the views spectacular, but the castle and the quarters of Papa Luna are fascinating. The surrounding city has many other

El Cid

People often associate the great Spanish knight El Cid with Peñiscola. It is a common mistake. The only connection is from the early 1960s, when the castle became the location for the Charlton Heston and Sophia Loren epic *El Cid*. The castle and surroundings played the role of Valencia but Peñiscola was never El Cid country. Nor, apparently, was it Sophia Loren country, as she never actually set foot here. The film was very good news for the castle and the city, which had run into disrepair. The Hollywood producers restored parts of the castle walls, both in and out, and refurbishment carried on after the film crews left.

buildings of interest, including the 15th-century Gothic and Romanesque parish church, **Iglesia de la Virgen del Socorro,** where you can see Papa Luna's chalice and processional cross, as well as other relics. The Artillery Store, *Parque de Artilleria,* now a botanical garden, has breathtaking views to the sea and to the beautiful Sierra de Irta Nature Reserve, a stunning 9mile/15km coastal mountain range stretching to the south of the town. ⏱ *2–3 hr. 93 miles/150km north of Valencia. Take the A7 (direction Castellon/Barcelona).*

Peñiscola.

2 Mandarina Restaurant, Terraza, Café. This place is a little of everything, and they do it very well. Fusion food complements stunning views across the beach to the castle. It is a café bar, too, and there's a terrace where you can listen to soothing chillout music. At night it becomes an indoor/outdoor club. *Avda Papa Luna 1.* ☎ *96-446-7650. $$$.*

3 ★★ Morella. Morella is the capital of Els Ports and is one of Spain's oldest towns, almost 1,000m/3,300ft

Practical Matters: Peñiscola & Morella

- **Tourist Information Office**: Plaza San Miguel, 3. Tues–Sat 9.00am–1.00pm and 4.00pm–8.00pm; Sun and Mon 9.00am–2.00pm ☎ 96-417-3032 www.morella.net.
- There are around 10 trains a day from Valencia to Benicarló/Peñiscola. The fast trains take around 70 minutes, and there is a slower, almost half the price service, which takes around half an hour more.
- **Lodging**: **Hotel Fábrica de Giner** (Ctra Morella–Corcall, km 4.5 ☎ 96-417-3142; www.fabricaginer.com) is part of a complex that was once a 19th-century textile factory; formerly the factory owner's home. Doubles cost 60€–86€. There's also a youth hostel with beds costing from around 6.60€ to half board at 11.50€. It has a restaurant and, across the road, a public swimming pool.

above sea level. Nothing can quite prepare you for the first view of this fairytale town: an outstanding example of a Medieval fortress that nestles below its crowning glory, the castle. The walls of the city are more than 2km long, punctuated by six entry gates and 14 towers. Inside the walls is a jumble of streets filled with tapas bars and restaurants, and shops selling everything from hams to woolly jumpers. The somewhat-ruined castle is a long, hot climb, but once there, not only do you get a feel of what it was like to live in the time of the Knights, but the views to

Morella.

Basilica de Santa María la Mayor.

the town below and across the countryside take your breath away. The 13th-century **Basilica de Santa María la Mayor** is the most beautiful church in the region. A Gothic array of saints and virgins around the two main doorways leads you inside. The gilt altar, the stained glass windows, and the spiral staircase leading to the unusual first-floor choir are among the treasures you will find. Particularly fascinating, for me at least, is the Baroque organ built in the 18th century, all gold and silver (including heavenly cherubs) with its 3,541 pipes. 🕐 *4–5hr. 135*

miles/218km north of Valencia. Take the A7 (direction Castellon/ Barcelona).

4️⃣ **Hotel Cardenal Ram.** Food in Morella is hearty and, in general, inexpensive. The restaurant in this hotel is no exception. Lamb or rabbit stuffed with truffle is a specialty of the house. Their menú degustación is worth the 25€ while their menú del día is even cheaper. *C/ Cuesta de Suñer 1.* 📞 *96-496-0911. www. cardenalram.com. $$.*

Morella's Museums

Morella's old town has several museums: Museo Tiempo de Historia (History Museum) at Portal de la Nevera, **Museo Tiempo de Imagen** (Photography Museum) at Torre Bebieto, which has old photos of the town, and **Museo Tiempo de Dinosaurs** (Dinosaur Museum) at Portal San Miguel. One more museum, **Museo Tiempo de Sexenni** in the Iglesia de Sant Nicolau, gives you an insight into the festival of the same name, held every six years (the next is 2012), a colorful festival of lively, confetti-strewn parades and decorated streets to celebrate the town's patroness, Virgen de la Villavana, who saved the town from the Plague in the Middle Ages. All the museums are worth visiting but my particular favorites are the photography and Sexenni museums. All are open 11am to 2pm and 4pm to 8pm and all have the same phone number, 📞 96-417-3128. Note: It is worth buying a combined 6€ ticket to the town's museums and the castle.

Gandia

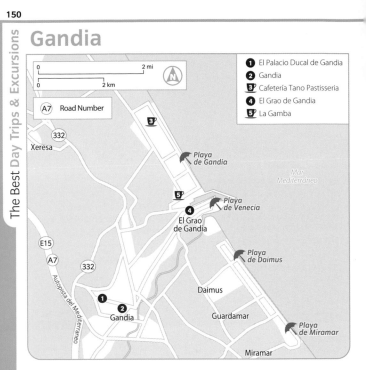

0 — 2 mi
0 — 2 km

(A7) Road Number

1 El Palacio Ducal de Gandia
2 Gandia
3 Cafetería Tano Pastisseria
4 El Grao de Gandia
5 La Gamba

(332) Xeresa

Playa de Gandia

Mar Mediterráneo

Playa de Venecia

El Grao de Gandia

(E15)
(A7)
(332)

Autopista del Mediterráneo

Playa de Daimus

1 2 Gandia

Daimus

Guardamar

Playa de Miramar

Miramar

South of Valencia are the wetlands of the Parque Natural de L'Albufera (see p 85), the Lagoon, and mile upon mile of rice paddies. Then, as you pass the seaside resort of Cullera, the scenery around you changes. Now, all you see are citrus groves, mainly oranges, known as Valencias and Valencia Lates, which fruit in late November and March. If you are lucky enough to visit at blossom time (April or December) the air is heavy and sticky-sweet with the fragrance. Gandia is at the center of these groves. **START: Drive 69km/ 43miles south on the Carretera A7 (direction Alicante).**

1 ★★ kids **El Palacio Ducal de Gandia.** Mention the name Borgia and most people automatically think of Italy and Papal corruption, but in fact he was a Valencian and bought the dukedom of Gandia for his family in 1485. *El Palacio Ducal de Gandia*, the 14th-century Ducal Palace of Gandia, is known to this day as the Palace of the Borja (Spanish for Borgia). Originally the main residence of the Royal Dukes of

Aragon, it remained in the Borja family until 1740. This fascinating building is well worth the trip to Gandia to see. It is a little unprepossessing from the outside but from the moment you enter the magnificent courtyard, *El Patio de Armas*, you know you are in for a treat. Like so many buildings from this period, it has been extended and restored many times, and is now a real hotchpotch of architectural styles,

Practical Matters: Gandia

- **Tourist Information Office**: Paseo Neptuno 45. ☎ 96-284-2407. www.gandia.es Open all year: Tues and Thurs 9.30am–2.30pm, Fri 9.30am–2.30pm and 3.30pm–6.30pm, Sun 9.30am–1.30pm.
- **By car from Valencia**, take the A7 in the direction of Alicante; the journey is 70km (44 miles). Frequent and cheap 'Cercanía' trains (every 30 minutes) leave from Valencia Estación del Norte and arrive in Gandia about an hour later. (☎ 902-24-02-02; www. renfe.es/cercanias).
- **Lodging**: There are some 24 hotels in Gandia, one three-star, and three hostels in the city. The rest are at the beach. The **Hotel Tano Resort** is a very recently modernized 1970s hotel. The rooms are fresh and comfortable, the gardens and pool are excellent, and there is a very good restaurant attached. (Pda. Redonda, s/n, 46730, Playa de Gandia. ☎ 96-284-5393; www.tanoresort.es; doubles 70€–102€ junior suites 137€–149€).

such as Gothic and 16th-century Renaissance. However, Baroque prevails, particularly so in the Gold Gallery, five highly decorated, gilded rooms separated by carved porticos—a stunning, almost over-the-top set of rooms with exquisite muralled ceilings. 🕐 *1 hr. C/ Duc Alfons el Vell, 1 46701 Gandia.* ☎ *96-287-1465. www.palauducal.com. Admission is by guided visit only: 2.50€, 1.50€ children, students, and seniors. Winter Tues–Sat 10am–1.30pm, 4.30–8pm. Summer, Tues–Sat 10am–1.30pm, 5.30–8.30pm; last tours 1 hour prior to closing.*

❷ ★ **The City of Gandia.** The city of Gandia is split into two halves. Inland is the commercial part, which also has a Medieval center that was once walled. This is where the Ducal Palace stands (see bullet ❶, p 150) along with the **Colegiata**, the 14th-century church of Gandia, which was burnt and sacked during the civil war but restored in the 1940s; the old university, founded by Saint Francesc de Borja in 1549 and still a school; the 15th-century Palacio Marqúes

González de Quirós, now a community and arts center; and the MAGa, a 14th-century building now housing the city's archeological museum. Much of the center is pedestrianized, with all the Spanish high-street chain stores. There are also some shady promenades, particularly Paseo de Germanias, and parks to walk or sit

Galeria Dorado, El Palacio Ducal de Gandia.

and relax in. ⏱ *2 hr. Tourist Information Office. A. Marques de Campo s/n. ☎ 96-287-7788. www.gandia.es. Open all year Mon–Fri 9.30am–1.30pm & 3.30–7.30pm, Sat 9.30am–1.30pm.*

3 Cafetería Tano Pastisseria. This is a local family-run chain in Gandia and we have been known to drive out of Valencia just to partake of one of their excellent multilayer sandwiches or a salad. We can never understand why they haven't stormed Valencia. For those with a sweet tooth, the patisseries are mouthwateringly tempting small works of art. *Paseo Germanies, 26 and there are six other locations around town.* ☎ *96-286-6917. $.*

4 ★ El Grao de Gandia. Until very recently, El Grao de Gandia was mainly frequented by Madrileños (citizens of Madrid) but is now being discovered by a more international visitor. As you drive to the beach you pass the pleasure boat marina, its quayside lined with busy bars, restaurants, and shops. Watching the sailing boats and motor yachts over a drink here is a very pleasurable way of passing the time. Cafés, amusement arcades, and ice cream stalls (and even an underground car park) line the promenade along this clean, sandy 6km-long beach. Kids enjoy the pedalos, while the grown-ups might like to try their hand at windsurfing or volleyball. And if you're a little more adventurous, there's a naturist section at the northern end of the beach. Gandia's thriving nightlife is legendary and has always been a major part of the draw for the city dwellers. Huge open-air nightclubs pump high-octane music into the early hours throughout the summer. ⏱ *half a day. Carretera A7 (direction Alicante) 69km/43miles from Valencia.*

5 La Gamba. This family-run restaurant (of Angel, his wife, Pilar, and their son and daughter Francisco and Pilar) is famous for inventing a pasta version of *Paella de Mariscos*, called *Fideua*. This is not necessarily true, even the family don't claim they invented it, but nonetheless the dish deserves every bit of the attention it receives. La Gamba is always busy but it is particularly packed on Sundays. Best to book. *Ctra Nazaret-Oliva s/n, Gandia.* ☎ *96-284-1310. $$$$.* ●

Gandia beach.

Before You Go

Spanish Government Tourist Offices

In the U.S.: 666 Fifth Ave., Fifth Floor, New York, NY 10103 (☎ 212/265-8822); 8383 Wilshire Blvd., Suite 956, Beverly Hills, CA 90211 (☎ 323/658-7188); 845 N. Michigan Ave., Suite 915E, Chicago, IL 60611 (☎ 312/642-1992); and 1221 Brickell Ave., Suite 1850, Miami, FL 33131 (☎ 305/358-1992). **In Canada:** 102 Bloor St. W., Suite 3402, Toronto, Ontario M5S 1M9, Canada (☎ 416/961-3131). **In the U.K.:** 22–23 Manchester Sq., London W1M 5AP (☎ 020/7486-8077).

The Best Times to Go

There is not really a bad time to travel to Valencia. The city has only recently begun to be a real tourist magnet and doesn't yet attract the crowds that Barcelona does. It is unlikely you will be overwhelmed by crowds of tourists for a while. The least attractive time to visit is August, not only because of the heat, which can be pretty daunting, but also because a great deal of the city closes as Valencians shut their bars, restaurants and shops to go on holiday.

Festivals & Special Events

Spain takes its fiestas, or bank holidays, very seriously. It is interesting that most fiestas fall on a Tuesday or Thursday. The Spanish often extend the break—they call it *El Puente* meaning 'the bridge'—by taking the intervening day of the weekend off too, giving them a four-day break. It is, you must admit, a great idea. Also worth noting is that many holidays are very local: certain towns will celebrate a holiday and businesses and stores will close, while others will remain hard at work.

Where possible I've quoted exact dates in this section but others are approximations. It's always best to check in advance, the Valencians like to surprise! A favorite expression here is *'Pensat i fet'*, literally meaning 'think and do', though it actually means 'immediately'. The longer my wife and I live here the more we realize the truth behind it. The Valencians, in particular, struggle with forward planning. It's not unusual for one of our Valencian friends to call at 10pm and suggest dinner at 11pm—and then on to a club, perhaps. Even big public events can be arranged in the same way. I often imagine conversations in government or corporate offices: 'Let's have a music festival!' 'When?' 'This Friday!' 'OK, I'll get on to it!'

Pensat i fet, always a surprise and why we love living here.

WINTER. **Fireworks Festival, October 8,** an enormous firework festival held in the Alameda, an hour of spectacular fireworks to celebrate Valencia Day.

Día de la Comunidad de Valenciana (Day of Valencia), October 9, a local public holiday to celebrate the conquest of Valencia by Jaime I (James 1) in 1238.

Día de la Hispanidad **(Spain Day), October 12.**

Día de Todos los Santos **(All Saints Day), November 1,** people visit the graves of their loved ones to lay flowers.

Día de la Constitucion Espanola **(Constitution Day).**December 6, a variety of cultural events are held to commemorate the day in 1978 when the Spanish approved the current constitution.

Noche Buena (Christmas Eve), December 24. Stores close from around midday as celebrations begin with a traditional family evening Christmas Eve meal. Almost every restaurant and bar closes and the city becomes almost a ghost town for the night; make sure you book dinner somewhere that is definitely open (or make friends with someone who will invite you to their home for a meal).

Navidad (Christmas), December 25, families tend to go out and eat in restaurants and then go for a walk along the promenade.

Noche Vieja (New Year's Eve), December 31, most people, particularly the under 30s, book themselves into *eventos*. These big evening-dress parties are held in hotels, clubs and discos and start around 1am and can cost up to 200€ a head!

The custom of *las uvas* is celebrated within the family where you eat 12 grapes in time to the chimes of midnight; only after this can you take to the streets and join friends at an *evento*.

Año Nuevo (New Years day), January 1, a *mascletà* (or daytime firework display with the emphasis on noise) in the Río Túria at 2pm.

Cabalgata de Los Reyes (The Three Kings Parade), January 5, a huge procession of the Three Kings, who land in the port/marina and process to the city joined by hundreds of floats. Go armed with plastic bags to catch all the sweets and toys thrown into the crowds.

Los Reyes (The Three Kings), January 6, traditionally the day Spanish children get their Christmas presents.

San Vicente Martir, January 22, the Patron Saint of Valencia is celebrated with religious and cultural processions.

Festival Veo, February, street performance and theatre from all over Europe. A week of surprises throughout the city and most entertaining.

Las Fallas, 15–19th March, see Arts and Entertainment page 122.

Toros (Bullfighting), March, Plaza de Toros–Placa de los Bous. Bullfighting is still very popular here and tickets sell out fast, especially for the more famous names. Fights only take place during fiesta times. The bullring is located next to the main station. Check www.tivlc.com for up-to-date information.

San Jose (Father's day), March 19.

La Magdalena, 3rd Sunday of Lent, Castellón (an hour's drive up the coast) has a celebration similar to Fallas, with parades, and fireworks, of course. Great to see if you miss *Fallas*.

SPRING. *Pascua* (Easter) *Semana Santa* (Holy week), solemn processions, throughout Holy Week, take place in Cabanyal's streets behind the beach. Penitents wear sinister-looking costumes with masked pointed hoods and floor length robes.

San Vicente Ferrer, Monday after Easter, stages are erected all over the city and short plays are performed by children.

Moros I Cristianos (Moors and Christians), around March 19, Valencia has these parades during Fallas but there are many more celebrations of Moors and Christians throughout the Comunidad. The very best and biggest is held in Alcoy, over three days, 21–24 April, and features noisy and entertaining mock battles. Other Moors and Christians parades are usually part of village fiestas. The costumes worn are remarkable, and cost a small fortune. There is a unique *Moros I Cristianos* walk, more of a swagger, which is something to be seen.

Cruces, 2nd or 3rd week in May, on the 2nd or 3rd week, you will come across floral crosses set up at crossroads and in front of churches, to celebrate the day of the cross, and a local competition takes place for the best cross.

Fiesta del Trabajo (Day of the Worker), May 1, a Trades Union parade takes place through the city.

La Virgen de los Desamparados (The Day of the Virgin of the Deserted or Forsaken), 2nd weekend in May, *Plaza de la Virgen,* begins Saturday evening with an open-air concert, and at least 400 costumed people dance into the Plaza at around midnight. Early Sunday morning, open-air *Misa* or Mass is delivered to a packed Plaza, after which it fills with more people than you can possibly imagine. The Virgen emerges from the main door of the Basilica, carried by several strong men, and the huge crowd surges, their aim to touch, kiss or make contact with this golden effigy. Babies, small children, even adults, are body surfed over the crowd in an attempt to touch her or her robes. It all lasts less than half-an-hour as she is carried to the Gothic door of the cathedral. On her short journey, people drop rose petals from their balconies over her.

Corpus Christi, 60 days after Easter, one of the most ancient of celebrations in Valencia, it has been celebrated since the 12th century. It is also known as Las Rocas, named after the extraordinary floats of animals, figures, and giants with their huge heads. These are brought out of the Casa de las Rocas museum (see p 19, bullet **6**) and paraded through the streets to the Plaza de la Virgen, where characters reenact biblical scenes. The procession continues through the Centro Histórico, past balconies decorated with tapestries and chandeliers put out for the event.

SUMMER. **Noche de San Juan (Night of St. John), June 23–24,** for this Mediterranean festival, everyone arrives at the beach carrying armfuls of wood and picnics; bonfires are lit and people of all ages gather round to party. The reason for this night is to jump into the waves at midnight. There are many stories: jump nine waves and make a wish, walk into the sea forwards and return backwards—or visa-versa. Another tradition is to write down the bad events of the year on a piece of paper and throw it in the fire, and finally jump the flames! The sight of all the bonfires as far as the eye can see is breathtaking and it is heartwarming to see everyone, young and old, celebrating together.

Bienial de Valencia, June– September, the next *Bienial* takes place in 2009. Valencia is awash with theater, dance, and exhibitions for this bi-annual arts exhibition.

Ferio de Julio **(July Festival), July,** punctuated each Saturday night throughout the month with a *Castillo*—fireworks on a grand scale. Wonderful concerts in Viveros, a Jazz festival at the Palau de la Música and other outdoor concerts, dances and events at parks throughout the city.

Batalla de las Flores **(Battle of Flowers), last Sunday of July,** on the last Sunday of July, a cavalcade of beautiful floats follows a route up and down the Alameda. On its second circuit, the crowd and the Falleras on the floats battle with Marigolds—until the street, and everyone on it, is covered with crushed petals. Followed by a Mascletá (The noisiest of daytime fireworks.).

Toros (Bullfights), July, it is fiesta time again, so time to catch a bullfight. Buy the more expensive *Sombra*, shade tickets, to make sure you are out of the sun. Sitting under the July sun at 3pm is not a good idea.

Festival Eclèctic, July, as the name suggests, an eclectic mix of music, dance, street theatre and arts in and around the spectacular grounds La Ciudad de las Artes y las Ciencias — and best of all, it's all free.

FIB (Festival Internacional de Benicàssím), 3rd week in July. An hour north by car from Valencia, FIB is Benicasim's answer to the UK's Glastonbury but without the mud—the only time you need to get wet here is if you go to the beach. This huge festival is one of the largest on the Med and attracts a bigger British audience each year. Good camping facilities are included in the ticket price and there are numerous hotels in this normally quiet resort, though they do get booked up very early. www.fiberfib.com.

La Filmoteca d'Estiu (Summer Cinema Under the Stars), July–early September, from the end of July through August in the gardens of the Palau, cult and classic films are screened in VOS (Original Version) by the IVAC. Most nights start at about 10 pm. Sit under the stars and enjoy.

La Tomatina, **last Wednesday in August,** Buñol, 45-minutes' drive from Valencia, holds this crazy festival. Basically, a tomato fight, 40tons of tomatoes are delivered by dumper trucks onto the streets and the crowd throws them at each other for exactly one hour. The locals are very hospitable and lay on hoses to wash down the tomato-soaked crowd. Now a world-famous event with almost 40,000 attending each year. Definitely not for the faint-hearted! www.tivlc.com.

The Weather

Valencia has a true Mediterranean climate: warm and humid summers and mild winters. January and February are the coldest months but temperatures rarely drop below 7°C/45°F and it is unlikely that you will ever see snow in the city. March and April are warmer with the sunny days getting longer. April, May and June are probably the best months, although late March and early April can bring some heavy showers. July, August and September are the hottest months with temperatures soaring to the above 30°C/86°F and at times it is very humid. October is very pleasant though there is sometimes torrential rain, and then in November and December it starts getting cooler. Nearly every day is sunny (300 days a year on average), and even when it rains, and you will certainly know about it when it does, it never lasts for more than a couple of days, and you can be sure another burst of sunshine is just around the corner.

Useful Websites

www.okspain.org: Tourist Office of Spain official U.S. site; it has detailed 'Before You Go' information (including U.S. air departures).

VALENCIA'S AVERAGE TEMPERATURE & RAINFALL

	JAN	FEB	MAR	APR	MAY	JUNE
Daily Temp. (°C)	17	18	19	21	24	27
Daily Temp. (°F)	63	65	66	70	75	80
Rainfall (cms/in)	2.2/0.86	2.8/1.1	2.3/0.9	3.2/1.26	3.2/1.26	1.7/0.67

	JULY	AUG	SEPT	OCT	NOV	DEC
Daily Temp. (°C)	30	31	28	24	21	18
Daily Temp. (°F)	86	88	82	75	70	65
Rainfall (cms/in)	0.6/0.24	0.8/0.3	4.8/1.88	4.9/1.92	4.0/1.57	2.6/1.02

www.spain.info: The official Spanish Tourist Office web site, a great website for both general and local information. www.spaininfo.com. Loads of practical tips on driving, destinations, bringing in pets, and even learning Spanish.

www.turisvalencia.com: The Official Website of Valencia city.

www.landofvalencia.com: The official tourism site of the Region of Valencia, this government run website has interesting articles and good listings for the region of Valencia.

www.thisisvalencia.com: One of the leading independent websites about Valencia, anything from what's on this week, where to buy a handbag or where to go for dinner.

www.valenciaterraimar.org: Not great English, but another useful website about mainly rural Comunidad Valencia.

www.renfe.es: The official site of Spanish rail, for routes, schedules, and booking.

Cell phones *(Móviles)*

World phones—or GSM (Global System for Mobiles)—work in Spain (and most of the world). If your cellphone is on a GSM system, and you have a world-capable multiband phone, you can make and receive calls from Spain. Just call your wireless operator and ask for 'international roaming' to be activated. North Americans can rent a GSM phone before leaving home from InTouch USA (☎ 800/872-7626; www.intouchglobal.com) or Road-Post (☎ 888/290-1606 or 905/272-5665; www.roadpost.com). There are various operators in Spain, and if you are in need of a Spanish number and sim card, it won't set you back a lot to buy one (you will need to take ID with you).

Car Rentals

Driving in Valencia is a little daunting to begin with but, with a little practice, is not so bad. Most hotels have underground parking or use of a nearby public car park. Various hire companies have their offices and pick up points at Estación del Norte in the centre of town, or the airport. The US giants **Avis** (☎ 96-152-2162; www.avis.es) and **Hertz** (☎ 96-152-3791; www.hertz.es) are here, and there are some very good and inexpensive smaller companies too: **Europcar** (☎ 96 152-1872; www.europcar.es) and **AurigaCrown** (☎ 96-152-6973; www.aurigacrown.com).

Getting **There**

By Plane

Valencia has a small, modern and easy airport. It is only x miles/8 km from the centre of town. If you are not hiring a car, the fastest and cheapest way (under 4€) is the Metro (subway); there are two lines to various points in the city but both end centrally at Xàtiva (Estación del Norte). (First metro 05:30am and last 11:00pm.) By bus, it is the Aérobus; it first leaves the airport at 5.25am and last at 23.55pm, dropping you off at the end of the Gran Via Fernando el Católico, just behind the Estación del Norte. It costs around 1.20€ and takes around 25 minutes to get into town, passing through a few villages on the way. Taxis are plentiful and cost around 15–20€ to the city, depending on traffic and the time of day. Valencian taxis are white, with a light on top, and if the light is green it means it's free.

By Car

The A-7, from France and Barcelona, swings around Valencia and then down to Alicante and on to the south of Spain. It is a three-and-a-half-hour fast drive from Barcelona and two hours from Alicante. The A-3 from Madrid to the city is around a three-hour fast drive.

By Train

Trains from Madrid and Barcelona arrive at Estación del Norte, the main train station(C/ Xàtiva, 24. ☎ 90-224-0202. www.renfe.es), as do all trains in and out of the city of Valencia.

By Boat

A car and passenger ferry runs to Valencia from Ibiza and Palma de Mallorca.

Getting **Around**

The Metro and Tranvía

Valencia's subway is clean and efficient. Its five different lines will take you around and out of Valencia. A single journey will cost you from 1.30€–4.35€, depending on where you are heading. A Bonometro is good value at around 6€ for 10 journeys around town; if you are planning on heading further out, make sure your Bonometro is valid for the right zones. If there are more than 15 of you traveling, there are group discounts available. First trains of the day are 5:30am and the last leave the main stations around 11:30pm. An extension of the subway is the Tranvía or tram service. On the north side of the old river bed, it extends from the Universities in the town of Burjasot, through the northern suburbs, across the top of the city, through the Politecnica and Naranjos faculties and all the way down and along the beach, forming the T-4 andT-6 (and part of T-5) lines of the metro. Though they look fairly space age, they are not the fastest way to get around, but useful to hop on and off when going to the beach.

By Taxi

All Valencian taxis are white, and these are three of the many official companies: Teletaxi ☎ 96 357-1313, Radio Taxi Valencia ☎ 96-370-3333 and Radio Taxi Manises ☎ 96-152-1155. Taxis are an inexpensive way of getting around, particularly if there are four of you, as the minimum charge in the daytime anywhere in Valencia is 3.60€, and after 10pm 6€. They run 24 hours a day. You will find taxi ranks all over the place, if you want to wait in line, but if like most Valencians you just want to wave a free one down, make sure it has a green light on top as these are licensed cab drivers.

By Bus

The Valencians love their buses. The network is amazing and most go through the Ayuntamiento (Town Hall Square) and past the Torres de Serranos. The EMT bus website shows all timetables and maps, and is very helpful (**www.emt valencia.es**.) Tickets, at 1.20€, can be bought from the driver, and the Bonobus, valid for 10 journeys, is available at most *estancos* (tobacconists).

For coaches up and down the coast, or inland, the bus station is on Avda Menéndez Pidal, ☎ 96-346-6266.

By Car

Parking in the city can be dreadful. You will notice lots of 'handbrake-off' double parking, thanks to too few parking meter places on the streets and not enough under-ground car parks. See p 158 for a list of rental car companies.

Valencia Tourist Bus

Valencia has a good jump-on, jump-off tourist bus service that tours the city all day, stopping at five main points. The tour, which takes one hour, starts at the Plaza de la Reina through Valencia, around the Ciudad les del Artes and back to the center. There is a soundtrack in eight lan-guages. Approximately costs 12€ for a 24-hour ticket, and there are dis-counts for children, senior citizens, and residents. (☎ 96-341-4400: www.valenciabusturistic.com).

Valencia Tourist Card

This is a great way to save money while traveling around Valencia. Choose one-, two- or three-day passes, giving you public transport for free and good discounts to museums, public buildings and the tourist bus. There are also discounts in many shops and restaurants for the cardholder. The card costs from 7€ to 15€, depending on card type. Easily available from hotels, newspa-per stands, tobacco shops and tourist offices.

Guided Tours

Many of the main museums and public buildings offer their own guides—usually, but not always, bookable in advance. There are sev-eral companies offering guided tours of the city by foot, and these are offered in several languages. **Valencia Guias** (☎ 96-385-1740 www.valenciaguias.com) is a good company offering all kinds of tours; individual, group, walking, cycling—they even offer tours on segways.

Check with the Tourist Information centers for a list of other companies.

Mobile Phone Guided Tours

A different way to tour the city! As you walk around, you will come across black and gold street **Museu Obert** signs positioned by a historic building or monument. Dial ☎ 650 800 200, the number on the sign, select your language, key in the number on the sign and enjoy a two-minute description of the loca-tion. There are 12 routes at the moment. Pick up details in the tourist offices. Calls are on a reduced charge, especially with Movistar phones. Calls are approxi-mately 18 cents a minute.

On Foot or By Bicycle

Valencia is a very walkable city: enjoy a stroll in the old river, up the Gran Vía Marqués del Túria, or just have a wander around and see where you come to. There are many cycle lanes in Valencia and various companies to rent bikes from. **Orange Bikes** on C/ Editor Manuel Aguilar, (www.orangebikes.net, ☎ 96-391-7551), have been around forever and have really helpful staff.

By Scooter

Just a couple of years ago the scooter made it big in Valencia. One of the first was **Cooltra** (Avenida del Puerto 47, ☎ 96-339-4751, www. cooltra.com), though it is now one of several companies. Cooltra offers plain old Scooter rental, or tours where you are, either a passenger riding pillion, or following a leader in a group. Whichever, it is a great way to see the city.

By Horse and Trap

You can pick up a horse and trap at the Plaza del Reina. It takes an hour, going around the historic centre, and costs approximately 30€. Seats four but is a very romantic trip for two. Just ask one of the horsemen.

Fast **Facts**

APARTMENT RENTALS   The up-and-coming thing in Valencia is to rent an apartment instead of staying in a hotel. The best picks are: **www.only-apartments.com,** an independent company that offer flats in every size, style and in every corner of Valencia. **www.friendlyrentals.com,** beautiful designer flats in the centre of town and **www.40flats.com,** a local company who offer clean, serviced apartments with reception.

ATMS/CASHPOINTS (CAJERO)   Most Spanish ATMs accept Maestro, Cirrus and Visa cards. You can exchange currency where you see the sign reading CAMBIO. **La Caixa** on La Plaza del Ayuntamiento is one of the biggest banks in Valencia and offers an English-speaking service and exchanges all types of currency. American Express is accepted at establishments where you see their sticker on the window. To pay by credit or debit card almost anywhere, you will be asked for some kind of photo ID.

BUSINESS HOURS   Banks open Monday to Friday, 8.30am to 2pm. Most large stores open around 9am and close at 9pm, and department stores are open from 10am to 10pm, Monday to Saturday. Smaller establishments still close from 2pm to 5pm for siesta time, and in August will often only open in the morning.

CONSULATES & EMBASSIES   **U.S Consulate,** Dr. Romagosa, 1, 2, J, Valencia (☎ 96-351-6973); **Canadian Consulate,** Núñez de Balboa 35, Madrid (☎ 91-423-3250); **UK Consulate,** Plaza de Calvo Sotelo, 1, 2º, Alicante (☎ 96-521-6190); **Australian Consulate,** Plaza Descubridor Diego de Ordás, Madrid (☎ 91-353-6600); **New Zealand**

Consulate, Pinar, 7, 3. Madrid (☎ 91-523-0226).

EMERGENCY NUMBERS   For any medical emergency or for an ambulance, dial ☎ 112, for police emergencies dial ☎ 080.

ELECTRICITY   Most hotels use 220 volts AC (50 cycles). It is very rare, but some older places only have 110 or 125 volts AC. If you feel it may be a problem, call in advance to make sure.

GAY & LESBIAN TRAVELERS   Valencia is the third gay capital of Spain, and is said to be one of the gay friendly cities of Spain. Same-sex marriage became legal in 2005, and in 1995 discrimination based on sexual orientation was banned. **www.thisisvalencia.com** have extensive listings of hotels, clubs, bars, cruising areas and anything and everything you need to know.

HOLIDAYS   Holidays observed include: January 1 (New Year's Day), January 6 (Feast of the Epiphany), March/April (Good Friday and Easter Monday), May 1 (May Day), May/June (Whit Monday), June 24 (Feast of St. John), August 15 (Feast of the Assumption), September 11 (National Day of Catalonia), September 24 (Feast of Our Lady of Mercy), October 12 (Spain's National Day), November 1 (All Saints' Day), December 8 (Feast of the Immaculate Conception), and December 25 (Christmas) and December 26 (Feast of St. Stephen).

INSURANCE   Check your existing insurance policies before you buy travel insurance to cover trip cancellation, lost luggage, medical expenses, or car rental insurance. For more information, contact one of the following recommended insurers: **Access America**

(☎ 866/807-3982; www.access america.com); **Travel Guard International** (☎ 800/826-4919; www. travelguard.com); **Travel Insured International** (☎ 800/243-3174; www.travelinsured.com); and **Travelex Insurance Services** (☎ 888/457-4602; www.travelex-insurance.com). For travel overseas, most U.S. health plans (including Medicare and Medicaid) do not provide coverage, and the ones that do often require payment for services upfront. If you require additional medical insurance, try **MEDEX Assistance** (☎ 410/453-6300; www.medexassist.com) or **Travel Assistance International** (☎ 800/821-2828; www.travel assistance.com; for general information on services, call the company's Worldwide Assistance Services, Inc., at ☎ 800/777-8710).

INTERNET Most hotels and hostals offer a wi-fi service, and if not, have computers you can use. You will also find various Internet cafés around the city. The biggest and best one is **ONO**, Calle San Vicente Mártir, 22 (☎ 96-328-1902. Look out for stickers in windows of bars and restaurants that offer wi-fi.

LOST PROPERTY Make sure you let your credit card company know immediately if you have had your wallet stolen or you have lost it, most credit card companies will ask for a police report (*denúncia*) so file one at the nearest police station. The emergency numbers for the U.S are; for **Visa** ☎ 800-847-2911, or 900-991-124 in Spain, **American Express** ☎ 800-221-7282 in the U.S., or ☎ 902-375-637 in Spain and **MasterCard** ☎ 800-307-7309 in the U.S., or ☎ 900-971-231 in Spain.

MAIL & POSTAGE The Spanish word for post office is *Correos* (koh-ray-os) and the main branch in the city is the Plaza Ayuntamiento

24 (☎ 902-197-197), and they are open Monday to Friday from 8am to 8pm, and Saturday mornings until noon. Stamps can be bought at *Estancos* (tobacconists) too, and are called *sellos* (say-yos). Post boxes are yellow and square, though many have been removed from the streets in the past few years.

MONEY Spain's official currency is the Euro. For up-to-date exchange rates between the dollar and the euro check out the currency converter website **www.xe.com/ucc**.

PASSPORTS UK, US and Canadian visitors do need a visa to visit Spain providing their stay does not exceed 90 days. Australian visitors do need a visa. If you lose or have your passport stolen, contact your country's embassy or consulate immediately (see p 161). Make sure you copy the critical pages of your passport and keep them in a safe place, separate.

PHARMACIES Pharmacies (*farmacia*) follow normal store opening hours, but there is always a *farmacia de guardia* that will stay open in each district on national holidays and during the night. You can find the location and telephone numbers of all of these on the doors of every pharmacy. You can also call ☎ 010 to contact all-night pharmacies.

POLICE In an emergency, call ☎ 091 for the national police and ☎ 092 for local.

SAFETY Valencia has a very low crime rate and tends to be a very safe city. As in all major cities, most pick pocketing and muggings happen in the tourist areas, so be more aware in busier places and especially near and in La Plaza de la Reina, Ayuntamiento, and Plaza de la Virgen. Have your wits about you and make sure you keep an eye on your belongings at all times. If something does happen to you, make sure you report it to the police.

SMOKING At the beginning of 2006 a new law was introduced in Spain, banning smoking in public places including public transport, hospitals, work places and hostelries. There are some bars and restaurants with no smoking areas, but these are usually very small and not too separate from the smokers. Many in Valencia still smoke, so if you really feel strongly about smoking and food, do phone ahead and ask if they have a *zona de no fumadores* (no smoking area).

TAXES The value-added (VAT) tax (known in Spain as IVA) ranges from 7 percent to 33 percent, depending on the commodity being sold. Food, wine, and basic necessities are taxed at 7 percent; most goods and services (including car rentals) at 13 percent; luxury items (jewelry, all tobacco, imported liquors) at 33 percent; and hotels at 7 percent. Non EU residents are entitled to a reimbursement of the 16 percent IVA tax on most purchases worth more than 90€ made at shops offering 'Tax Free' or 'Global Refund' shopping. Forms, obtained from the store where you made your purchase, must be stamped at Customs upon departure. For more information see **www.globalrefund.com**.

TELEPHONES For national telephone information, dial ☎ 11818. For international telephone information, call ☎ 11825. To make an international call, dial ☎ 00 and the country code, area code, and number. To place a call to anywhere in Spain, you must first dial the two-digit city code; 96, for example, for Valencia and the Valencian community, then the seven-digit number.

TIPPING Very few people here tip more than a few coins, even in the better restaurants. For coffees and snacks most people just leave a few coins or round up to the nearest euro. Taxis do not expect tips.

Tip hotel porters and doormen 1€ and maids about the same amount per day.

TOILETS In Valencia, the names on the doors can be baffling—toilets can be called any of the following: *aseos*, *servicios*, *baños* and *lavabos*. Women should look for the words *señoras*, *damas*, *dones* or even *Luna* (with an image of the moon), while men should head straight for *caballeros*, *homes* or *Sol* and an image of the sun. There are very few public toilets in the city but there is an unspoken rule that cafés and bars allow free use of their services unless they specify otherwise.

TOURIST INFORMATION There are several official tourist information offices in the city. On Plaza de la Reina ('Reina', Plaza de la Reina 19. ☎ 96-315-3931; www.turisvalencia.es) and in the Ayuntamiento (Town Hall), they offer information on only the city. The large office on La Paz, ('Paz', C/.Paz 48. ☎ 96-398-6422, www.comunitatvalenciana.com) offers information on both the city and the whole community, as does the office in Poeta Querol (Diputación (Town Hall), Poeta Querol s/n. (Teatro Principal) ☎ 96-351-4907, www.valenciaterraimar.org).

TRAVELERS WITH DISABILITIES Conditions for persons with disabilities are slowly improving in Valencia. Newer hotels are more sensitive to the needs of the disabled, and more restaurants are becoming generally wheelchair-accessible. Both transport networks, the metro and bus, are wheelchair-accessible. There are elevators and ramps in most central Metro stations and buses are equipped or adapted for wheelchairs. Many metro stations are also now adapted to help travelers with visual impairments too, with Braille and audio information as well as tactile surfaces. The official tourist website www.turisvalencia.com has a very good section on 'Accessible Valencia' in the sub-menu of the 'Discover Valencia' section, giving lots of further information on monuments, the city, and tours for people with reduced mobility.

Valencia: **A Brief History**

138 B.C. The City of 'Valentia' is founded by Junios Brutus Roman soldiers; it was destroyed by Pompey and then rebuilt.

304–711 A.D. Christianity comes to Valencia; Martyrdom of San Vicente Mártir. Collapse of Roman Empire, Valencia becomes Visigoth and goes into decline again.

711–1088 Moors take over Valencia and over centuries, Valencia flourishes. The Moors and Muslims have the greatest effect on the growth of Valencia, trading in olives, rice, oranges, paper, silk, glass, gold and ceramics. The most important legacy is the irrigation system, which is still in use today. Several structures remain from these times, namely El Miguelete, said to have been the steeple on the old mosque, the Cathedral, The Baños del Almirante and the Portal de Valldigna.

1087 El Cid conquers Valencia; Christian re-conquest of Spain.

1238 Jaime/Jaume I (James I) of Aragon re-conquers Valencia for the Christians and founds the Kingdom of Valencia. Some 50,000 Moors are forced to leave.

1356 The new city wall is constructed.

1390–1411 Sometime between these dates Saint Vincent Ferrer converts so many Jews to Christianity he is allowed to take over their synagogue for his new Hospital San Salvador.

1492 *Queen Isabella*, sailed by Columbus, sets off financed by Valencian Bankers, and discovers the Americas.

13TH C. Christians, Muslims and Jews live together in Valencia quite peacefully at this time and work on the Cathedral begins in 1262.

14TH–15TH C. Golden age for Valencia, with huge growth of agriculture, industry, art, architecture and education, and becomes known as one of the major cities in the Mediterranean.

1609 Massive economical and political collapse after the Moors and the Jews are expelled, taking a wealth of skilled workers from the silk and agriculture areas with them.

1808–1813 Napoleonic armies march into Spain and the French army occupies Valencia for a brief period.

1865 City wall demolished to expand the city; only two towers remain today, Torres de Serranos and Torres de Quart.

1936–39 Spanish Civil War. During this time, the Republicans set up temporary government in Valencia.

1936–75 Franco Regime. Following the Civil War, Franco bans the teaching and speaking of Valenciano (this has been completely reversed today, every child is required by law to learn Valenciano).

1957 The great flood of the city and the decision to move the river-bed.

1975 Death of Franco and the restoration of democracy under Juan Carlos, who is crowned the new King of Spain. Comunidad Valenciana became an autonomous state. Valencia has had an extremely rapid growth both economically and in the tourist sector. A massive building program goes under way, which is still taking place today.

1990S TO PRESENT DAY Valencia's huge building program includes the Palau de Música (Music Palace), Ciudad de las Artes y las Ciencias, (City of Arts and Sciences) and the new marina. In the 1980s Valencia is under a left-wing government, in 1991 it swings to the right, and a conservative government is still in power today.

2006 Pope Benedict visits Valencia for the fifth Catholic World Meeting of Families.

2005–2008 World-renowned sporting events, Louis Vuitton Cup, America's Cup and Formula 1 European Grand Prix all held in Valencia.

2009 The Spanish Tennis Open comes to Valencia.

Valencia's **Architecture**

Roman (10th century)
Some ruins from the original city when founded in 138 B.C. and from the later, Visigoth period, can still be found in and around the Centro Histórico, particularly in Plaza L'Almoina.

First Romanesque (11th century)
'First Romanesque' or 'Lombard Romanesque' from Lombardy in Italy develops into Second Romanesque, bulky and heavier in design. Examples can be seen in the city in the Puerta del Palau of the Cathedral moldings, the door onto Plaza de la Virgen.

Gothic (13th–15th century)
Natural light is introduced through grander windows and columns, and moldings become more elegant as space and light becomes a key element. There are numerous examples in Valencia, the most outstanding being La Lonja de los Mercaderes, Torres de Serrano and Quart and the Cathedral tower, El Miguelete.

Renaissance (15th–16th century)
The more elaborate design of previous centuries is replaced by simple, symmetrical and classic lines, as a great interest in ancient Greek and Roman architecture develops. A magnificent example is El Convento del Carmen.

Baroque (17th–18th century)
The taste for the classical loses its appeal, and architecture once again becomes more decorative. A new, theatrical style introduces curves and twisting outlines where the straight, understated columns stood. Light and perspective are greatly manipulated, seen in Valencia's main entrances to the Cathedral and the Iglesia de los Santos Juanes. A completely over-the-top, extreme variation of the Baroque is Churrigueresque, clearly visible in the stunningly elaborate facade of the Palacio del Marques de dos Aguas.

Neoclassical (mid-18th–19th century)
After the overly ornate and frivolous style of the Baroque, a return to the purity of ancient architecture is born, yet more decorative than the Renaissance. Fine examples are the **Plaza de Toros,** reminiscent of a Roman coliseum, and **The Ayuntamiento** (Town Hall) and **Correos** (Post Office) buildings.

Modernismo/Modernista (late 19th–early 20th century)
A variation of what you and I would call Art Nouveau, Antoni Gaudi was the Catalunian/Spanish pioneer in this brand new look—colorful ceramics, glass and gorgeous sweeping lines make up the aesthetic style. The **Mercado de Colón** is a perfect example, now restored to its former

glory, as are the **Mercado Central** and **Estación del Norte**.

Modern & Contemporary (1960–present)

Santiago Calatrava is said to be partly responsible for the city's new-found fame. His distinctive architecture as seen particularly in the space age La Ciudad de las Artes y las Ciencias (see p 19, bullet ❽) is now world famous.

There are many other fine examples of very modern architecture: Norman Foster's Palau de Congresos completed in the late 1990s and José María de Paredes' wonderful greenhouse-like Palau de la Música (see p 117), which opened in 1987. More latterly, the surprisingly majestic Veles e Vents (see p 13, bullet ❷) building by British architect David Chipperfield with b720 Arquitectos of Barcelona. Many more fine and monumental buildings are planned for the city over the next few years, some of which will open in 2009 including Estadi Nou Mestalla (see p 119) and Calatrava's latest El Ágora (see p 24, bullet ❻).

Useful Phrases & Menu Terms

Useful Words & Phrases

ENGLISH	SPANISH/VALENCIÀ	PRONUNCIATION
Good day	Buenos días/ Bon dia	*bweh*-nohs *dee*-ahs/ bohn *dee*-ah
How are you?	¿Cómo está?/ Com està?	*koh*-moh es-*tah*/ com ehs-*tah*
Very well	Muy bien/Molt bé	mwee byehn/mohl beh
Thank you	Gracias/ Gràcies	*grah*-thee-ahs/ *grah*-see-ehs
You're welcome	De nada/De res	*deh nah*-dah/deh ress
Goodbye	Adiós/Adéu	ah-*dyos*/ah-*deh*-ooh
Please	Por favor/ Per favor	por fah-*vohr*/ pehr fah-*vohr*
Yes	Sí/Sí	see
No	No/No	noh
Excuse me	Perdóneme/ Perdoni'm	pehr-*doh*-neh-meh/ per-*don*-eem
Where is . . . ?	¿Dónde está . . . ?/ On està . . . ?	*dohn*-deh es-*tah*/ ohn ehs-*tah*
To the right	A la derecha/ A la dreta	ah lah deh-*reh*-chah/ ah lah *dreh*-tah

ENGLISH	SPANISH/VALENCIÀ	PRONUNCIATION
To the left	A la izquierda/ A l'esquerra	ah lah ees-*kyehr*-dah/ ahl ehs-keh-*ra*
I would like . . .	Quisiera/ Voldría	kee-*syeh*-rah/ vohl-*dree*-ah
I want . . .	Quiero/Vull	*kyeh*-roh/*boo*-wee
Do you have . . . ?	¿Tiene usted?/ Té vosté?	tyeh-neh oo-*sted*/ te voss-*teh*
How much is it?	¿Cuánto cuesta?/ Quant és?	*kwahn*-toh *kwehs*-tah/ kwahnt ehs?
When?	¿Cuándo?/Quan?	*kwahn*-doh/kwahn
What?	¿Qué?/Com?	Keh/Cohm
There is (Is there . . . ?)	(¿)Hay (. . . ?)/Hi ha? or Hi han?	aye/ee ah/ ee ahn
What is there?	¿Qué hay?/Que hi ha?	keh aye/keh ee ah
Yesterday	Ayer/Ahir	ah-*yehr*/ah-*eehr*
Today	Hoy/Avui	oy/ah-*wee*
Tomorrow	Mañana/Demá	mah-*nyah*-nah/deh-*mah*
Good	Bueno/Bo	*bweh*-noh/boh
Bad	Malo/Roin	*mah*-loh/roh-*in*
Better (Best)	(Lo) Mejor/ Millor	(loh) meh-*hohr*/ mee-*yohr*
More	Más/Mes	mahs/mehss
Less	Menos/Menys	*meh*-nohs/*meh*-nyus
Do you speak English?	¿Habla inglés?/ Parla anglès?	ah-blah een-*glehs*/ pahr-lah ahn-*glehs*
I speak a little Spanish/ Catalan	Hablo un poco de español/ Parle un poc de Valencià	ah-bloh oon *poh*-koh deh es-pah-*nyol*/ pahr-leh oon pok deh vah-lenh-see-*yah*
I don't understand	No entiendo/ No entenc	noh ehn-*tyehn*-doh/ noh ehn-*tehnk*
What time is it?	¿Qué hora es?/ Quina hora és?	keh *oh*-rah ehss/ *kee*-nah *oh*-rah ehss
The check, please	La cuenta, por favor/ El compte, per favor	lah *kwehn*-tah pohr fah-*vohr*/ ehl *cohmp*-tah per fah-*vohr*
the station	la estación/ la estació	lah es-tah-*syohn*/ la ehs-tah-*ssyo*
a hotel	un hotel/ unhotel	oon oh-*tehl*
the market	el mercado/ el mercat	ehl mehr-*kah*-doh/ ehl mehr-*kaht*
a restaurant	un restaurante/ un restaurant	oon rehs-tow-*rahn*-teh/ oon rehs-tow-*rahn*
the toilet	el baño/el bany	ehl *bah*-nyoh/ehl bah-ny
a doctor	un médico/ un metge	oon *meh*-dee-koh/ oon meht-*jeh*
the road to . . .	el camino a/ al cami a	ehl kah-*mee*-noh ah/ ehl kah-*mee* ah

ENGLISH	SPANISH/VALENCIÀ	PRONUNCIATION
to eat	comer/menjar	ko-*mehr*/mehn-*jahr*
a room	una habitación/	*oo*-nah ah-bee-tah-*syohn*/
	un habitació	oon ah-bee-tah-*syoh*
a book	un libro/	oon *lee*-broh/
	un llibre	oon *yee*-breh
a dictionary	un diccionario/	oon deek-syoh-*nah*-ryoh/
	un diccionari	oon deek-syoh-*nah*-ree

Numbers

NUMBER	SPANISH	VALENCIANO
1	uno (*oo*-noh)	un (oon)
2	dos (dohs)	dos (dohs)
3	tres (trehs)	tres (trehs)
4	cuatro (*kwah*-troh)	quatre (*kwah*-treh)
5	cinco (*theen*-koh)	cinc (sink)
6	seis (says)	sis (sees)
7	siete (*syeh*-teh)	set (seht)
8	ocho (*oh*-choh)	huit (weet)
9	nueve (*nweh*-beh)	nou (noo)
10	diez (dyehth)	deu (*deh*-ooh)
11	once (*ohn*-theh)	onze (*ohn*-zeh)
12	doce (*doh*-theh)	dotze (*doh*-tzeh)
13	trece (*treh*-theh)	tretze (*treh*-tzeh)
14	catorce (kah-*tohr*-theh)	catorza (kah-*tohr*-zeh)
15	quince (*keen*-seh)	quinza (*keen*-zeh)
16	dieciséis (dyeh-thee-*says*)	setze (*seh*-tzeh)
17	diecisiete (dyeh-thee-*syeh*-teh)	disset (dee-*seht*)
18	dieciocho (dyeh-thee-*oh*-choh)	dihuit (dee-*weet*)
19	diecinueve (dyeh-thee-*nweh*-beh)	dinou (dee-*noh*-ooh)
20	veinte (*beyn*-teh)	vint (vihnt)
30	treinta (*trayn*-tah)	trenta (*trehn*-tah)
40	cuarenta (kwah-*rehn*-tah)	quaranta (kwah-*rahn*-tah)
50	cincuenta (theen-*kwehn*-tah)	cinquanta (theen-*kwahn*-tah)
60	sesenta (seh-*sehn*-tah)	seixanta (see-*shahn*-tah)
70	setenta (seh-*tehn*-tah)	setanta (seh-*tahn*-tah)
80	ochenta (oh-*chehn*-tah)	vuitanta (vwee-*tahn*-tah)
90	noventa (noh-*behn*-tah)	noranta (noh-*rahn*-tah)
100	cien (*thyehn*)	cent (sent)

Menu Terms
Meals & Courses

ENGLISH	SPANISH	PRONUNCIATION
Breakfast	Desayuno	deh-sah-*yoo*-noh
Lunch	Almuerzo	al-*mwehr*-thoh
Dinner	Cena	*theh*-nah
Meal	Comida	ko-*mee*-thah
Appetizers	Entremeses	en-treh-*meh*-sehs
Main course	Primer plato	*pree*-mehr *plah*-toh
Dessert	Postre	*pohs*-treh

Table Setting

ENGLISH	SPANISH	PRONUNCIATION
Glass	Vaso	*bah*-soh
	or Copa	*koh*-pah
Napkin	Servilleta	sehr-vi-*lye*-tah
Fork	Tenedor	teh-neh-*dor*
Knife	Cuchillo	koo-*chee*-lyoh
Spoon	Cuchara	koo-*chah*-rah
Bottle	Botella	boh-*teh*-lyah
Cup	Taza	*tah*-thah

Decoding the Menu

ENGLISH	SPANISH	PRONUNCIATION
Baked	Al horno	ahl *ohr*-noh
Boiled	Hervido	ehr-*vee*-thoh
Charcoal grilled	A la brasa	ah lah *brah*-sah
Fried	Frito	*free*-toh
Grilled	A la plancha	ah lah *plan*-chah
Rare	Poco hecho	*poh*-koh *eh*-choh
Medium	Medio hecho	*meh*-dyo *eh*-choh
Well done	Muy hecho	mwee *eh*-choh
Roasted	Asado	ah-*sah*-thoh
Sauce	Salsa	*sahl*-sah
Spicy	Picante	pee-*kahn*-teh
Stew	Estofado	ess-toh-*fah*-doh

Dining Out

ENGLISH	SPANISH	PRONUNCIATION
Check/bill	Cuenta	*kwen*-tah
Waiter	Camarero *(masc.)*	kah-mah-*reh*-roh
	Camarera *(fem.)*	kah-mah-*reh*-rah

Assorted Foods
Beverages

ENGLISH	SPANISH	PRONUNCIATION
Beer	Cerveza	thehr-*veh*-thah
Coffee	Café	kah-*feh*
Milk	Leche	*leh*-cheh
Pitcher	Jarra	*hah*-rah
Tea	Té	teh
Water	Agua	*ah*-gwah

ENGLISH	SPANISH	PRONUNCIATION
Wine	Vino	*bee*-noh
Red	Tinto	*teen*-toh
Rosé	Rosado	roh-*sah*-thoh
White	Blanco	blahn-*koh*
Wine list	Carta de vinos	*kahr*-tah deh *bee*-nohs

Meat, Sausages & Cold Cuts

ENGLISH	SPANISH	PRONUNCIATION
Beef	Buey	*bway*
Duck	Pato	*pah*-toh
Meat	Carne	*kahr*-neh
Chicken	Pollo	*po*-lyoh
Cold meat	Fiambre	*fyam*-breh
Cutlet	Chuleta	choo-*leh*-tah
Ham	Jamón	hah-*mohn*
Cooked ham	Jamón York	hah-*mohn* york
Cured ham	Jamón Serrano	hah-*mohn* seh-*rah*-noh
Lamb	Cordero	kohr-*deh*-roh
Kidneys	Riñones	ree-*nyoh*-nehs
Liver	Hígado	*ee*-gah-thoh
Partridge	Perdiz	*pehr*-deeth
Pheasant	Faisán	fahy-*thahn*
Pork	Cerdo	*thehr*-doh
Rabbit	Conejo	koh-*neh*-hoh
Ribs	Costilla	kos-*tee*-lyah
Sausage	Salchicha	sahl-*chee*-chah
Spicy sausage	Chorizo	choh-*ree*-thoh
Steak	Bistec	*bee*-stehk
Sirloin	Solomillo	so-loh-*mee*-lyoh
Tripe	Callos	*kah*-lyohs
Turkey	Pavo	*pah*-voh
Veal	Ternera	tehr-*neh*-rah

Seafood & Shellfish

ENGLISH	SPANISH	PRONUNCIATION
Anchovy		
salt	Anchoa	ahn-*choh*-ah
fresh	Boquerón	boh-*keh*-rohn
Bass	Lubina	loo-*bee*-nah
Bream (porgy)	Besugo	beh-*soo*-goh
Cod	Bacalao	bah-kah-*lah*-oh
Crab	Cangrejo	kan-*greh*-hoh
Crayfish	Cigala	see-*gah*-lah
Cuttlefish	Jibia	*hih*-byah
Fish	Pescado	pess-*kah*-thoh
Flounder	Platija	plah-*tee*-hah
Hake	Merluza	mehr-*loo*-thah
Grouper	Mero	*meh*-roh
Lobster	Langosta	lahn-*goss*-tah
Mackerel	Caballa	cah-*ba*-lyah

ENGLISH	SPANISH	PRONUNCIATION
Monkfish	Rape	*rah*-peh
Mussel	Mejillón	meh-hee-*lyohn*
Octopus	Pulpo	*pool*-poh
Oyster	Ostra	*ohs*-trah
Prawn	Gamba	*gahm*-bah
Red mullet	Salmonete	sal-moh-*neh*-teh
Salmon	Salmón	sal-*mohn*
Sardine	Sardina	sahr-*dee*-nah
Scallop	Peregrina	peh-reh-*gree*-nah
Shellfish	Mariscos	mah-*reess*-kohs
Sole	Lenguado	len-*gwah*-tho
Shrimp	Camarón	ka-mah-*rohn*
Squid	Calamar	kah-lah-*mahr*
Swordfish	Pez espada	*peth* ess-*pah*-thah
Trout	Trucha	*troo*-chah
Tuna	Atún	ah-*toon*
Turbot	Rodaballo	roh-dah-*ba*-lyoh

Vegetables & Legumes

ENGLISH	SPANISH	PRONUNCIATION
Carrot	Zanahoria	thah-nah-*oh*-ryah
Cabbage	Col	kohl
Red cabbage	Lombarda	lom-*bahr*-dah
Celery	Apio	*ah*-pyoh
Chickpea	Garbanzo	gahr-*bahn*-thoh
Corn	Maíz	mah-*eeth*
Eggplant	Berengena	beh-rehn-*jeh*-nah
Fava (broad) beans	Habas	*ah*-bahs
Green beans	Judías	hoo-*dee*-yahs
Lentil	Lenteja	lehn-*teh*-hah
Leek	Puerro	*pweh*-roh
Lettuce	Lechuga	leh-*choo*-gah
Mushroom	Seta	*seh*-tah
Potato	Patata	pah-*tah*-tah
Pumpkin	Calabacín	kah-lah-bah-*theen*
Salad	Ensalada	enn-sah-*lah*-dah
Spinach	Espinaca	ess-pee-*nah*-kah
Onion	Cebolla	theh-*bo*-lyah
Tomato	Tomate	toh-*mah*-teh
Vegetables	Verduras	vehr-*doo*-rahs

Recommended **Spanish Wines**

I recommend seeking out the following wines while touring Spain.

Reds (Tintos)
Rioja Viña Ardanza, Allende, Imperial, CVNE, Marqués de Riscal, La Rioja Alta, San Vicente, Castillo de Ygay, López Heredia, Muga, Remírez Ganuza, Roda, Artadi

Riber del Duero Reds   Condado de Haza, Pago de los Capellanes, Emilio Moro, Pesquera, Hacienda Monasterio, Aalto, Atauta, Alíon, Mauro, Leda, Vega Sicilia
Toro   Quinta Quietud, San Román, Dos Victorias, Pintia, Numanthia
Priorat   Cims de Porrera, Clos Martinet, Clos Mogador, Mas Doix, Vall Llach, L'Ermita
Jumilla   Casa Castillo, Finca Sandoval
Monsant   Celler de Capçanes, Joan d'Anguera
Utiel-Requena (Valencia)   Vincente Gandia, Primitivo Quiles, Pago de Tharsys, El Miracle
Others   Dominio de Valdepusa/Marqués de Griñón (Toledo), Castillo de Perelada (Penedès), Chivite (Navarra), Dominio de Tares (Bierzo), Torres (Penedès)

Whites (Blancos)
Ablariño (from Galicia)   Lagar de Cervera, Laxa, Martin Codax, Terras Gaudia, Pazo de Señorans
Rioja   Muga, Marqués de Riscal, López-Heredia
Rueda   Dos Victorias José Pariente, MartinSancho, Belondrade y Lurton

Other
Cava (sparkling) Catalonia   Agustí Torelló, Avinyó, Gramona, Juvé y Camps, Segura Viudas
Utiel-Requena (Valencia)   Torre Oria
Sherry   San León (manzanilla), Tío Pepe (fino), Alvear (Pedro Ximénez)

Recommended Vintages for **Rioja & Ribera del Duero** Wines

YEAR	RIOJA	RIBERA DEL DUERO
1990	Good	Excellent
1991	Average	Average
1992	Good	Good
1993	Average	Fair
1994	Outstanding	Excellent
1995	Outstanding	Outstanding
1996	Excellent	Outstanding
1997	Good	Good
1998	Excellent	Excellent
1999	Excellent	Excellent
2000	Excellent	Excellent
2001	Outstanding	Outstanding
2002	Average	Average
2003	Good	Good
2004	Outstanding	Outstanding
2005	Excellent	Very good
2006	Very Good	Good
2007	Very Good	Very Good

Toll-Free Numbers **& Websites**

AER LINGUS
☎ *800/474-7424 in the U.S*
☎ *01/886-8844 in Ireland*
www.aerlingus.com

AIR CANADA
☎ *888/247-2262*
www.aircanada.com

AIR FRANCE
☎ *800/237-2747 in the U.S.*
☎ *0820-820-820 in France*
www.airfrance.com

AIR NEW ZEALAND
☎ *800/262-1234 or -2468 in the U.S.*
☎ *800/663-5494 in Canada*
☎ *0800/737-000 in New Zealand*
www.airnewzealand.com

ALITALIA
☎ *800/223-5730 in the U.S.*
☎ *8488-65641 in Italy*
www.alitalia.com

AMERICAN AIRLINES
☎ *800/433-7300*
www.aa.com

AUSTRIAN AIRLINES
☎ *800/843-0002 in the U.S.*
☎ *43/(0)5-1789 in Austria*
www.aua.com

BMI
No U.S. number
☎ *0870/6070-222 in Britain*
www.flybmi.com

BRITISH AIRWAYS
☎ *800/247-9297 in the U.S.*
☎ *0870/850-9-850 in Britain*
www.british-airways.com

CONTINENTAL AIRLINES
☎ *800/525-0280*
www.continental.com

DELTA AIR LINES
☎ *800/221-1212*
www.delta.com

EASYJET
No U.S. number
www.easyjet.com

IBERIA
☎ *800/772-4642 in the U.S.*
☎ *902/400-500 in Spain*
www.iberia.com

ICELANDAIR
☎ *800/223-5500 in the U.S.*
☎ *354/50-50-100 in Iceland*
www.icelandair.is

KLM
☎ *800/374-7747 in the U.S.*
☎ *020/4-747-747 in the Netherlands*
www.klm.com

LUFTHANSA
☎ *800/645-3880 in the U.S.*
☎ *49/(0)-180-5-838426 in Germany*
www.lufthansa.com

NORTHWEST AIRLINES
☎ *800/225-2525*
www.nwa.com

QANTAS
☎ *800/227-4500 in the U.S.*
☎ *612/131313 in Australia*
www.qantas.com

SCANDINAVIAN AIRLINES
☎ *800/221-2350 in the U.S.*
☎ *0070/727-727 in Sweden*
☎ *70/10-20-00 in Denmark*
☎ *358/(0)20-386-000 in Finland*
☎ *815/200-400 in Norway*
www.scandinavian.net

SWISS INTERNATIONAL AIRLINES
☎ *877/359-7947 in the U.S.*
☎ *0848/85-2000 in Switzerland*
www.swiss.com

UNITED AIRLINES
☎ *800/241-6522*
www.united.com

US AIRWAYS
☎ *800/428-4322*
www.usairways.com

VIRGIN ATLANTIC AIRWAYS
☎ *800/862-8621 in continental U.S.*
☎ *0870/380-2007 in Britain*
www.virgin-atlantic.com

Index

See also Accommodations and Restaurant indexes, below.

Accommodations Index

Photo **Credits**

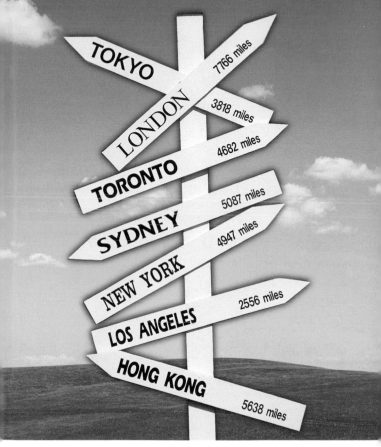

Explore over 3,500 destinations.

TOKYO — 7766 miles
LONDON — 3818 miles
TORONTO — 4682 miles
SYDNEY — 5087 miles
NEW YORK — 4947 miles
LOS ANGELES — 2556 miles
HONG KONG — 5638 miles

Frommers.com makes it easy.

Find a destination. ✓ Book a trip. ✓ Get hot travel deals.
Buy a guidebook. ✓ Enter to win vacations. ✓ Listen to podcasts.
Check out the latest travel news. ✓ Share trip photos and memories.
And much more.

Frommers.com

day BY day

Get the best of a city in 1, 2 or 3 days

Day by Day Destinations